THE
OUTSIDER
ADVANTAGE

THE OUTSIDER ADVANTAGE

*Because You Don't
Need to Fit In to Win*

CIERA ROGERS

PORTFOLIO | PENGUIN

Portfolio / Penguin
An imprint of Penguin Random House LLC
penguinrandomhouse.com

Most Portfolio books are available at a discount when purchased in quantity
for sales promotions or corporate use. Special editions, which include personalized
covers, excerpts, and corporate imprints, can be created when purchased in
large quantities. For more information, please call (212) 572-2232 or email
specialmarkets@penguinrandomhouse.com. Your local bookstore can also assist
with discounted bulk purchases using the Penguin Random House corporate
Business-to-Business program. For assistance in locating a participating retailer,
email B2B@penguinrandomhouse.com.

LIBRARY OF CONGRESS CATALOGING-IN-PUBLICATION DATA
Names: Rogers, Ciera, 1987– author.
Title: The outsider advantage :
because you don't need to fit in to win / Ciera Rogers.
Description: [New York] : Portfolio/Penguin, [2024] | Includes index.
Identifiers: LCCN 2023054615 (print) | LCCN 2023054616 (ebook) |
ISBN 9780593332429 (hardcover) | ISBN 9780593332436 (ebook)
Subjects: LCSH: Rogers, Ciera, 1987– | Fashion designers—
United States—Biography. | Success in business.
Classification: LCC TT505.R648 A3 2024 (print) |
LCC TT505.R648 (ebook) | DDC 746.9/2092 [B]—dc23/eng/20231208
LC record available at https://lccn.loc.gov/2023054615
LC ebook record available at https://lccn.loc.gov/2023054616

Printed in the United States of America
1st Printing

Book design by Alissa Rose Theodor

Map illustrations by Alexis Farabaugh

For Mom

CONTENTS

Road Map

SUCCESS

NOTE: If you can follow this road map to success precisely, without wavering from it for even an instant, you will most definitely, unequivocally, without a doubt achieve . . . a massive migraine. Banging your head onto a wall will likely ensue. Proceed with caution.

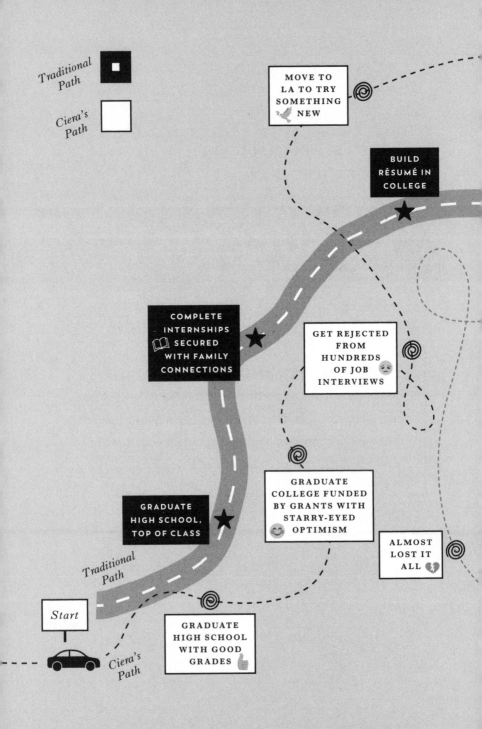

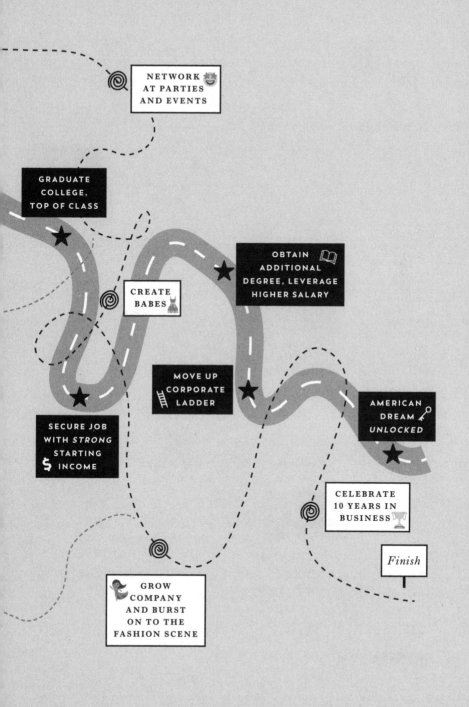

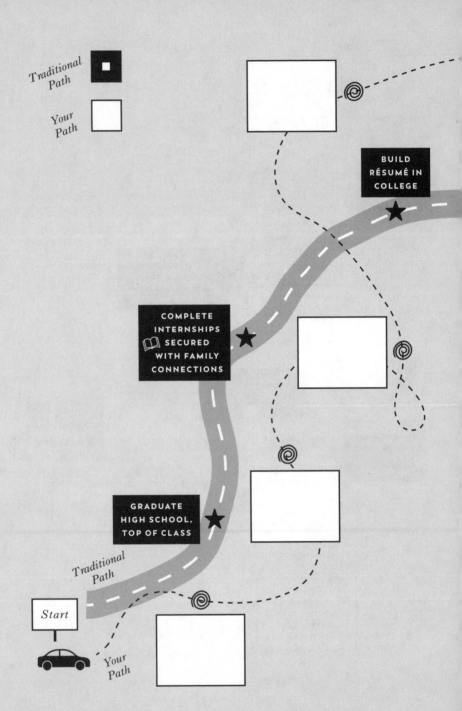

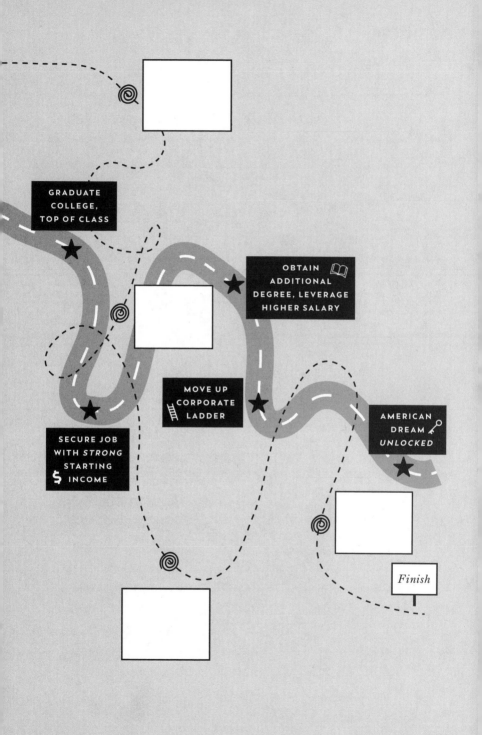

Introduction

WHY LISTEN TO ME?

Don't listen to me.

Listen to you.

I wish I could fill these pages with a foolproof guide or blueprint for success for you to follow like a recipe. But there isn't one. And don't trust anybody who tells you there is. Success doesn't work like that. If you don't believe me, turn back a page and follow the little car along that map again.

Success is personal. Success takes different shapes. It's not a straight line, as the world would have you believe.

Instead of telling you blow by blow how to make something of yourself, *The Outsider Advantage* is going to take you on a journey—my journey—of discovering how I dug into myself and used my differences to build lasting success by starting my own business. And doing so against impossible odds: I started Babes, my multimillion-dollar fashion business, when I lived on a borrowed couch with ten bucks to my name and no family or support system to fall back on. I did it all without a fancy business degree, credentials, or corporate experience. Instead, I leaned into the unconventional life experience I *did* have to unlock game-changing potential, and Babes grew from a word-of-mouth social selling venture to an international brand worn by Kim Kardashian, Lizzo, and more.

You will have a front-row seat as I unpack moments in my life that left huge marks on me and would influence my future—like how in high school "home" was sometimes my mother's red jeep and how being kidnapped at three years old ended up being one of the most challenging yet powerful experiences I've endured, overcome, and used to propel me forward. You'll hear about the highs and lows of entrepreneurship, when I went to my first Hollywood party, when Beyoncé made me feel seen, the six months when I ran my business while basically living in a hospital, when I made my first million, and the moment I almost lost it all overnight. I hope in showing you my meandering journey—and how I've used the things people often see as disadvantages as fuel to create something big—*The Outsider Advantage* will inspire you to accept yourself for who you are, use your experiences no matter how different they might be from your peers' or from what is considered "normal," and confidently chart your own course.

This book can't guarantee you'll become a millionaire or that your wildest dreams will come true overnight. It also isn't going to erase the traumatic scars from things you've lived through. What it is going to do is give you a searchlight to shine in those dark corners to unearth *gems*—memories, moments, pain, obstacles, trauma, experiences, differences—that you can use to build success in your life! Because there *is* treasure there. And believe me: I'm going to help you mine that shit.

THE
OUTSIDER
ADVANTAGE

1

Harness the Power of What's in Your Closet

AFFIRMATION

I have untapped power

In 2012, when I moved to Los Angeles with nothing but the clothes on my back, I realized the American dream was bullshit.

The idea that there was a level playing field of opportunity and because of that I could accomplish what anyone else could felt impossible to wrap my mind around as I sat on my roommate's couch, stomach churning. My head throbbed. I couldn't remember the last time I'd eaten. Coffee could hold a person for only so long. I eyed the ten-dollar bill in my purse. I skimmed the top shelf where my roommate kept *her* food. My shelf, below it, was bare. It was late summer and I—the first college graduate in my family—was bumming it rent-free on the couch in a friend of a friend's one-bedroom apartment. Several weeks earlier I'd bought a one-way ticket from Houston. My plan was simple: get an entry-level job in public relations. But, several weeks later, I still had nothing to show for myself.

I'd just turned on the faucet when a key slipped in the door. Stacy, my roommate, strode in.

"Hey," I said.

"So?"

My brow cinched in confusion.

"Look, Ciera, you're my girl but I need you to start helping me pay the rent."

My heart knocked against my ribs. I swallowed, on edge at the exasperated bite in her tone. "I'm trying to find something."

"I know, but . . ." She scrubbed a palm down her face. "I need half by the end of the month or I gotta find someone else to take your place." She walked past me into her room while I stood there, shocked. Before she closed her bedroom door, she tucked her lips in a sympathetic smile. "Girl, I can't afford this place on my own. I need you to find a way." The door closed.

The world tipped sideways. It was the fourth of August. Half of the rent was one *thousand* dollars. I had ten dollars. Her words replayed in my head over and over. I gulped down a dry breath, trying to slow my racing pulse. How was I going to get that much money? That fast? This was Stacy's place. She'd moved to Los Angeles from Houston years before I had. This wasn't personal. She couldn't carry me. Nor did I expect her to. When Stacy offered me her couch, I agreed to cover part of the rent. Now I actually had to do it . . . in less than a month.

I fell back onto "my" couch and checked my phone to see if there were any side job postings I'd missed. Since my PR job applications had gotten zero bites, I started taking styling gigs to make a little cash. But swiping through that day, there was nothing new posted and no job application responses in my email.

Twenty-six days.

One thousand dollars.

Or I would be homeless *again*.

This time in a city where I knew no one.

Uprooting myself to move to Los Angeles was an impossible decision, but when Houston began to feel like being on a hamster wheel, I couldn't lie to myself anymore—staying there was a dead end. I remember one interview in the late afternoon at a hotel in southwest Houston. I dressed in a mismatched skirt suit with a low-cut, '70s-style blazer. The skirt was dark blue and a bit worn at the hem. The blazer was gray with black stitching. It wasn't designer or even department store, but it's what I had. Beneath the blazer was a basic black top. I'd found the whole ensemble at a thrift store for a few bucks. I got all my clothes, for as long as I could remember, from thrift stores because they were cheaper than Walmart and Kmart. But as soon as I sat down, the hiring manager's gaze darted from my face to my outfit. The mood at the table shifted. She smiled, tucking a strand of blond hair behind her ear. I was applying for an entry-level corporate position, but she looked at me as if my attire suggested I was applying for a part-time job at Hot Topic. (No shade to Hot Topic. I look back on my goth phase with glee.) After introductions, she dove straight in.

"You don't have any experience working in hotels?"

"I don't." *I've never even stayed in one*, I thought.

"Well." She cleared her throat. "Tell me a bit about what you could bring to a marketing position here." She narrowed her eyes ever so slightly. I could *feel* the conclusion she'd already drawn in her head about me. I wasn't getting this job. Just like I hadn't gotten the dozen others I'd interviewed for weeks before. It appeared I had two choices: refuse to waste my time and walk straight out of that hotel and not look back, or go through the motions, clinging to hope that *this* time I would be wrong. I sat up in my seat, looked her right in the eye and said, "I know how to convince people to spend money better than anyone."

She met my eyes. I had her attention now.

"It's all about messaging. A brand makes a promise to a potential customer. Anyone who sees this place or visits your website should get the impression that staying here is an experience they *crave*."

"Anyone?" Her brow raised. "Our target mark—"

"Your market is bigger than you think. Whether someone has the money to stay here isn't relevant. If people want something bad enough, they'll find the money. You're missing an entire segment of income if you're only marketing to those who can afford you."

Her stare roved my resume again. "And how do you know all this?"

I eyed my watch. That question was presumptuous and disrespectful. Why did the *how* matter? I cleared my throat, warring with how honest to be. How much of me to let her see. Perhaps I hadn't shown enough of myself in other interviews? I sat straighter and met her eyes, rubbing my clammy hands on my skirt. *Here goes nothing.*

"I'm . . . innovative and clever."

Her lips pursed.

"For example." I leaned in. "After this interview, I'm taking a gentleman, to a strip club where I have an agreement in place with a group of strippers to ensure he spends an exorbitant amount of money on them. Afterward, the girls and I split the proceeds fifty-fifty."

She guffawed; her cheeks flushed. The rest of the interview was lackluster. I didn't get the job, big surprise. The rejection email was something about how I lacked traditional marketing experience. They encouraged me to reapply after I'd done a few internships. I don't know if she believed my strip club hustle or not, but I wasn't lying. I'd done it a handful of times when I was desperate for cash. After college, I made money however I could because I was stubborn, resourceful, creative, hardworking—and *broke*. (Not the kind of broke where I can't splurge on my favorite wine once a month. I'm talking about the kind of broke where hot water is how you lull your empty stomach to sleep.)

My inability to find a job in Houston wasn't for lack of trying or laziness. There was a lack of opportunity for someone like me, with a degree but no experience in the industry I wanted to go into. I'd expanded my search from top PR firms to companies with any sort of marketing department. If they had a job listing, I was applying. After a while, if the job posting for a business position even mentioned the words "entry level," I clicked APPLY. But like the hotel interview, they all wanted internship experience. In 2012, most internships were unpaid. Those that did offer pay usually offered a small stipend, but they required long hours, making it difficult to have a job as well.

I didn't have the privilege of working for free.

Because I needed to work to eat.

While in college in Houston, I worked different jobs, styling people with their own wardrobes, delivering items, helping out at a retail store for a few hours each week, and hosting at a nightclub. I took whatever work I could find while carrying a full academic course load and maintaining straight As. But I never accumulated enough cash to do anything besides pay rent and utilities, keep my cell phone on, and help my mom with whatever she might need. I juggled ten thousand balls as a full-time student, assuming that once I walked across that graduation stage, things would be different. I dreamed of finding a job that suited my natural talents. I was *good* at marketing. Instinctually. But here I was, months after graduating, degree in hand, and being turned down at yet another job interview. Forced to rely on stretching cash from my side hustles. This wasn't the life I wanted. The idea of college had been shoved down my throat by every guidance counselor, community group leader, and teacher for as long as I could remember. I followed the steps, graduated with a perfect grade point average, and it amounted to nothing more for me than dead-end jobs and no time (or energy) left to build anything sustaining. I did all the firstborn things and yet this American dream I'd been promised was ever elusive.

So I set my sights on LA, hoping to find a PR job that better aligned with my skills and actual experience, which was in the fashion industry: working retail, styling wardrobes, buying for stores, and vintage thrifting. Los Angeles was the fashion mecca, so I thought I might have a better shot at landing something there. I knew I could pick up small jobs to sustain myself if needed, as I had in Houston. I had nothing to lose in moving. I packed a small bag, told my mom goodbye, and stuffed all the money I had into my pocket—two hundred dollars. When the plane took off, I could hear the whir of the wheels folding up. The plane bobbed in the air and for a moment I felt weightless, as if I didn't have a care in the world. I imagined myself, arms stretched wide, flying with my own wings to a new future in a new place where I could marry my knack for fashion and my dream of working in PR. For a moment, I was full of hope. Until I wasn't.

Soon after I arrived in Los Angeles, I realized my college degree wasn't a magical key that opened a bunch of doors in this city either. None of the jobs I applied for were calling me back. The meager money I did manage to make was from meeting up with aspiring photographers and helping put together their models' outfits. But styling gigs didn't pay much. Less than a hundred dollars here and there, maybe. To be clear, I wasn't a high-maintenance, disillusioned, bratty twenty-two-year-old looking for the job of my dreams to snatch me up with nothing to offer in return. I had skills to offer, I wanted to make money, and I was going to take whatever job I could find to get me there, no matter how hard I'd have to grind. I was no stranger to hard work, overwork, impossible work, uncomfortable work. I was—and still am—the hardest-working person I know.

But as I sat on Stacy's couch, two months in, all I could think about was the collection of nos I'd gotten there. I'd been turned down for job after job in Los Angeles as well. And here I had no strip club connection, no retail store or club front to work in. My styling cash wasn't enough. Just like being the first in my family to graduate from college wasn't enough. Being a model student and child, despite home and food insecurity, wasn't enough. The work experience I did have wasn't enough. Doing all the things I was supposed to do on paper wasn't enough to create a good start or any sort of real sense of success in my life. It was beginning to feel like *I* wasn't enough. The walls felt like they were closing in. What did I have to show for any of the things I'd accomplished? A borrowed couch, good marketing instincts, a brain brimming with ideas, and a closet full of cute clothes that I'd thrifted?

I'd tried *everything*, I thought.

But I was wrong.

Just then, my Instagram pinged. I had a comment on a photo I'd posted of me in a cute thrifted outfit. Suddenly a memory of working part-time for my mother at a thrift store she started while I was in college tugged at me like an anchor.

Once a customer came into the store looking for something to wear to a concert. She wanted something unique that no one else would be seen in. Mom was on a phone call, so I helped her. The customer was tall with narrow hips and a flat chest. She wanted something to accentuate the little curves she had. I pulled out a man's button-down dress shirt and laid it to the side.

"You don't want to look like you're in a costume," I told her. She watched with her eyes wide as I draped her in a fur vest before tossing it and trying a black sequin top. Then swapping that for a sequin *dress* instead. This dress had a little more stretch in the fabric. It was bright blue and, depending on the light, the sequins would shine green. But because of how tightly it was stitched, it wasn't as gaudy as the bright pink. I held it up to her. Sometimes I had to just see it to know it would look right.

"Put this dress on over that shirt," I said, gesturing to the button-down I had pulled out earlier.

"Over? As in, on top?" She blinked.

"Yep."

She sized me up, eyed my own clothes, and took a deep breath, deciding to trust me. When she put the dress on, I adjusted the way it hung on her, flaring the bottom and widening the collar so it showed a bit of her skin. Not only did she buy that outfit, but she bought boots to go with it. The shirt had a vintage flair that could be played up or down. But the dress gave it a more modern appeal.

Ultimately, though, she bought it because she saw unique pieces reworked to create something fresh, different, new. Something no one else would be wearing. *That's* what I'd created for her. That's what she wanted. *That's* what Mom's store was selling—an experience of stepping out somewhere and knowing no one will look like you.

I sunk deeper into Stacy's couch realizing I could do this online. My mother found customers by wearing her own outfits in public and then by word of mouth from satisfied clients. I didn't have a community in Los Angeles. No one was talking about me. Yet. But I did have access to a potentially large audience online.

And the best part was that I had tons of uniquely styled outfits that I had made.

Stacy's words still buzzed through me. My gaze snapped to my "closet," which was a few inches of rod space in the entryway with a bunch of board games. Dangling there was a black bodysuit, a patterned dress I'd chopped in half and made into a skirt and a top, a pair of jeans I'd slit on the side and cut holes in, and a handful of other pieces I'd carted around over the years.

I pulled out the stretchy, long-sleeve bodysuit. It was a dated afterthought when I found it on a rack for six bucks at a thrift store. But I cut off the sleeves and hand sewed the edges the best I knew how (read: terribly). I removed the thick belt so it showed a bit of skin at the waist. Then, I slit the legs from the knee down to better show off a colorful heel. I slipped into the bodysuit. It was really cute. It fit like it was made for me, hugging my wide hips, cinching at my narrow waist.

I pulled open the curtains and light poured into our tiny apartment. I dragged Stacy's floor mirror and set it beside the window to bounce the light and brighten the room. Then I stacked a bunch of magazines on top of a stool to prop up my phone. I set the camera timer, posed, and snapped a picture. I took a few more to get a few different looks. I'd decided to post this outfit on Instagram for sale. The tagline would be simple: "body-con suit, sixty dollars." My hand shook as I typed the post. I'm not sure if it was in anticipation or fear that I could be out of my mind, wasting the little time I had on something that was impossible. Selling clothes on Instagram?! Could this really work?

I thought back to Mom. She spent most of her life flitting from pillar to post, struggling to build stability for me and my younger sister. But when I was in college, she opened her retail store for a while where she sold thrifted looks, and she was so happy. Her store was different from other retail stores because she was selling outfits that she made herself from scraps she'd purchased from resale clothing stores. And my mother styled clothes in an unusual way that evoked originality.

Others in the thrifting business would select a decade and dress within that. Sixties style, for example. But my mother never picked one decade. Instead, she mixed looks from different decades and maintained a modern flair. She'd take a dress that suited the current style and layer a few pieces with it, a top that felt more '70s and perhaps gloves that harkened back to the '50s. It was unusual but unique. And Mom sold it like couture. Everything I knew about styling I learned by watching her.

I realized it's not what you have in your closet, it's how you use it.

At first glance, the bodysuit I'd found in that resale shop looked like no more than a frumpy old disco outfit. But I could *see* the way it would fit perfectly at the waist and how, without sleeves, I could layer it with a sheer long sleeve. Where others saw an outdated '80s all-in-one jumpsuit in faded fabric with stains on the arms and frayed hems, I saw what it could be, just like my mom could. Sitting on Stacy's couch I realized I could *see* that same potential in myself. Just as I saw it in clothes.

Perhaps that was the battle I was having over and over with interviewers. They were looking at my "closet" of skills and translating it as not good enough. But I had a *lot* in my closet: skills, experiences, a lot of know-how that textbooks didn't teach.

I reflected on my experiences: thrifting because I was too poor to buy clothes elsewhere, refusing to waste anything, stubbornly continuing to apply for jobs in an industry that didn't want me. And I saw ingenuity, resourcefulness, resilience, tenacity. Despite living on a borrowed couch with ten dollars to my name, I had potential. I didn't know how long poverty would be a monkey on my back. But I was capable of so much more. And staring at my closet right then, I'd never felt anything so strongly.

I decided at that moment that I would be successful.

By using what I *did* have.

Suddenly the resume I'd held on to so tightly with a mangled mix of embarrassment (because of how little it actually did for me) and pride (because of how much I'd overcome to get it) felt like *just* a piece of paper. It didn't define me or sum me up. Just as being turned down time and time again for jobs I knew I could do quite well didn't sum up who Ciera Rogers would be. Their short-sightedness did not determine my potential. I did.

You do.

Hitting a "success wall" in my hometown and uprooting to a new place without anyone or anything and *actually* surviving under-scored how I saw myself and what I'd bring to the table from then on. In my closet, I had clothes that I'd stitched and sewed to mix and match, which I ultimately used to launch a million-dollar fashion brand. Success for me was in getting off my friend's couch, being able to stand on my own two feet, and finding stability. Success for you might be starting your own business, or getting the promotion you've always wanted, or breaking into an industry that feels out of reach. Or perhaps the success you crave has nothing to do with a career at all. Maybe the looming carrot you feel like you can't ever get your grip on is revolutionizing your health, finding a way to travel the world, figuring out how to juggle the *endless* demands of stay-at-home-mom life without feeling like you're doing *none* of it well. Or maybe you don't have a family or even a partner yet, but you'd like to eventually build the family you never had. Whether your goals are professional or personal, the first step toward succeeding at them is still the same: open your "closet" and harness the power of what's in there. Remember, most big things start with a tiny idea.

You might have pockets of time, a broad network of connections in a particular field, a knack for baking, or a gaming talent that on the surface seems like a waste of time. Or maybe you're warm; people naturally gravitate toward you; or you're annoyingly positive, expertly analytical, or argumentative. You'd be surprised what you can do with what you have. Resist hyperfocusing on how far you are from the success you're trying to build and start looking at the resources and skills at your fingertips. That's how you set yourself up to win! Consider the experiences you've had, the knowledge you've passively acquired, the ways you naturally excel. Pull *those* T-shirts out, slit them down the sides, tilt your head a bit, maybe step back to get some perspective. And put it back together.

Building the success that you've longed for starts with using what you have.

And you have *a lot* more than you realize.

———

Not long after I posted the picture from Stacy's couch, notifications on my phone started going off. Most comments on my picture were just saying how cute I looked. I didn't have a big following at the time, only a few hundred people. Still, this would work. I could feel it in my gut. At the end of the string of comments was the one that forever changed the trajectory of my life.

Jazzigirl82: I'll take it! How do I buy?

The outfit I'd bought for six bucks sold for sixty dollars. I was in business.

Stepping into this radically powerful new perspective of recognizing all the things in my closet wasn't easy. How'd I do it? I'll give you *not* the inside, but the outside (see what I did there?) scoop on what worked for me in case it helps you:

THE OUTSIDE SCOOP

I Ignored That Inner Demon
Who Says I Don't Have Shit

There is this little gremlin that lives in my head, and it's a complete hater. It works overtime to convince me that I cannot do whatever it is I am about to do. I had to learn to recognize that voice as the liar that it is, try to ignore it, and then try to shut it up altogether. That voice was really my own insecurity keeping me from chasing my wildest dreams. To counter that voice whenever it started to speak up, I decided to arm myself with an affirmation I'd say to bat it away. I'm a big believer in affirmations. It is transformatively powerful to fill your mind with self-affirming words of encouragement. At the time I was job hunting, I used the affirmation: *I have untapped power.*

I said it to myself over and over out loud at the start of my day as I sought out new opportunities. And I repeated it to myself in the quiet moments after I got a rejection and slowly but surely that nagging, nay-saying voice became harder and harder to hear. If any of this resonates with you, you have to ask yourself, What are you passively convincing yourself you're not capable of? In each chapter, I'll be sharing an affirmation that helped me in a particular season in my life in the hopes it will serve as an inspiration to you as well, whether you choose to adopt the same affirmation, a similar one, or something totally different but perfectly suited for you.

I Explored the Relationship Between What I'm Good at and What I'm Passionate About

The hardest part of figuring out what type of work I should earnestly pursue was figuring out what made the most sense. I knew there were industries and fields of work that I was genuinely interested in. But was I good at those things? On paper it appeared I didn't make the cut. So, I made two lists and compared them. The first list was of things I am good at naturally. Instinctual things such as digesting large amounts of information at a time without getting overwhelmed, and a whole host of other random things such as putting my makeup on without a mirror and with my eyes completely closed, and feeding myself with a fork using only my toes. (When you really let yourself freely write *all* the things you can do, the list can get wacky, in the best way!) I can also do money-related math in my head calculator-fast. Then there were things like sizing women's bodies and putting together cute outfits, which don't require much conscious labor. It's like I was pre-wired with these fashion-oriented abilities thanks to my experience growing up around my mother. But for years I didn't look at fashion designing or styling as an actual career choice. They are so second nature to me that I took them for granted.

The other list I made was of all the things I'm passionate about, the things that make me perk up and smile, the "work" I could do for hours and never make a dime but *love* it. On that list is film, music and art, among other things. In the margins I jotted down notes on what sorts of hard skills are required to do such jobs. For example, I am passionate about film production and one of the hard skills required is video editing (which I don't possess).

When I finished my lists, I compared them and looked for talents that supported my passions and vice versa. I also made a note of hard skills I didn't have but could acquire. This process opened up my mind to possibilities I hadn't ever considered and ultimately changed the trajectory of my work life. I immediately saw a connection between my love of beautiful things and my eye for fashion. I could see a path forward: designing clothes—a form of art—that made people feel beautiful.

What talents do you have that are so second nature you don't really think of them as hard skills? How do those intersect with your experiences so far and the goals you've carved for yourself?

2

Make Money Without Having Any

AFFIRMATION

I have plenty to build from

'm addicted to getting things for free.

Even now, I get this nauseous feeling in my gut when I have to spend *actual* money. So when I was dead broke, spending any money at all was like rubbing sandpaper on my skin. I was determined to build this business as inexpensively as possible. I had so little, it was a stretch of my imagination to even fathom how I could build anything. But, within a week of my first piece selling on Instagram, I'd posted three more outfits. They were each a bit different, uniquely thrifted, each flattering to curvy shapes, designed to hug all the right places and make any female feel fabulous and confident in their body. Each of those three outfits sold within hours. I had found my niche.

After I sold my first piece, I managed to find a part-time job at a clothing resale shop, but it paid $200 per week, which even for someone bad at math is obviously *not* going to equal $1,000 in rent by month's end. Still, it was something. I was committed to continuing thrifting outfits and posting them on Instagram to keep as much money as possible coming in. Every dollar helped. The clock was ticking.

One afternoon after a four-hour evening shift, I hitched a ride across town to the thrift store and grabbed two pairs of pants and a couple shirts. It was 8:00 p.m. when I got home. But my workday was far from done. My collection of plastic grocery bags underneath the couch was growing by leaps and bounds. I pulled out my bags of clothes, needles, thread, safety pins, and spare buttons and spread them all out. I wanted to post four outfits that week, which was going to take some organizing and planning.

After about an hour of ripping apart a jacket and messily pinning the jagged edges of fabric to look like a hem, I slipped it on. If I sucked in my breath just so, the pins would hold long enough for a picture. Holding absolutely still, with all the nerves and anticipation, it felt like a rock was on my chest as I checked my clothes. Once I was sure the jacket fit properly enough to be nicely photographed, I set it aside and prepped another outfit. But by midnight I only had two outfits ready. The next morning before work I took pictures, and on my way to work I edited them to brighten them up a bit and add a little contrast. Then I posted them for sale on Instagram. I worked a full shift. When I got off, my manager handed me $200, my pay for the week.

"Are you all right? You seemed distracted today."

"I'm fine," I replied robotically.

By the time I was on my way home, each item had a comment from a buyer ready to pay. I made $140 selling those two outfits in a matter of hours. *If I could repeat that process . . .* My heart squeezed as I pulled out my needle and thread after reviewing the buyers' measurements. I hand sewed the pinned hems until they looked neat enough to be passable. Then I hustled to ship everything out that same evening.

I counted my cash. It had been sevenish days since Stacy's ultimatum, and I had $410. Up from $10.

"I'm going to have your money," I told Stacy when she came home that night. I still wasn't entirely sure I would, but it was more of a promise to myself and her. I could see that I was onto something.

"Great," she said.

I'm sure she was wondering how. But the how didn't matter. My business was technically off the ground. It was just a bit raggedy.

Now I just had to keep this going . . .

My eyes were heavy, but I wanted to get another series of outfits up immediately. Time was a commodity I could not afford to waste. I flipped through a dozen hangers, trying to pick clothes I didn't mind parting with. I grabbed a skirt that I'd slit thigh-high up the side and paired it with an oversized top that I'd cut to give it a wide neck, exposing one shoulder. I modeled it myself and posted. Well past midnight, I checked my phone one last time. I had a buyer. She'd left a message with her measurements, her shipping address, and a request to make the neckline wider because she had a larger bust.

My shift at the store was in six hours. But I dragged myself up and pulled out the outfit to start sewing. An hour later I rechecked my phone and realized I had a message from her saying she thought she'd commented on the second outfit I posted that day and wanted to be sure she was ordering the right item. My heart sank. The second outfit was sold, gone. I had been taking down an outfit after it sold, so I wasn't sure how this mix-up happened. She'd already sent me money via PayPal, which had taken out its fees. So, I crossed my fingers and sent her pictures of the outfit I was in the process of sewing, and to my great relief she liked it, agreeing to purchase that one instead. But on this one, she *didn't* want the neckline wider because it was already off shoulder. I groaned. I'd already cut the fabric. But I told her I'd finish it up and get it to her ASAP.

I stayed awake that night determined to fix the neckline of that dress, but as I tried to sew back the edges of the wider neck hole, I zigged when I should have zagged, stabbed my finger, and ripped the fabric. Blood dripped down my hand. I bit into my fist and every expletive I've ever heard ran through my mind. It was 2:30 a.m., and this was a shirt I'd bought from a thrift store. There was no replacement.

My heart pumped faster, blood pooling in my ears. I paced. I couldn't afford mistakes, time wasted, resources lost. A sewing machine would be great. A proper place to store and organize things would be even better. A way to properly take orders—a dream! But I had nothing to build a legitimate business from. I was starting from scratch.

Or so I thought.

I texted the customer *again* in the middle of the night and explained that I needed a bit more time to ship her order. The next morning, I called my job and said I'd be late. I'm never late. Anywhere. But in that moment that job paled in comparison to the future I was convinced I was stitching together with the fabric in my hands. I hightailed it to the thrift store and pored through those aisles until I found a comparable replacement for the top. It wasn't the same material, but it was the same color. I rushed to work. And rushed through work. Afterward, I sewed the hem of the cut top properly and shipped it out to her. The stress between my shoulders unclinched a little as I left the post office. But my heart still pounded. I ended up only profiting $20 on her outfit.

The next few days were spent biting my nails, waiting for her to respond saying how she didn't like it. She ended up posting a picture of her wearing it a week later with the caption, "It looked a bit different online, but super cute. Go check out @cierarogers y'all."

I slumped over in relief, then burst out laughing. I didn't even have a business name, yet—ha! Raggedy was an understatement.

In the clear with that customer, I began to pump myself up to hit the ground running on my routine and do it all over again the next day. But I sank into Stacy's couch with a familiar sagging frustration. I felt like I had something big. I could feel it. But as someone who didn't come from financial privilege, someone squarely on the outside socioeconomically, without proper resources—it was *hard* to bring it to fruition. It felt impossible to keep it going with the day job. And yet, I had to do it to make ends meet. I also *wanted* to do it because it felt good to build something. Really good. But every move I made seemed to erect some new obstacle in my way, making things twice as hard for me—someone with nothing—than anyone else, it seemed.

I'd felt this feeling before.

I was eight years old and playing basketball with some kids down the street one afternoon. My mom and I lived in an apartment that her boyfriend at the time helped her pay for. My sister and I had followed some neighborhood kids to the park while my mom was at work. They tossed the ball in my direction, and I caught it awkwardly. Something popped and my finger twisted sideways. Dangling there. *Broken.* My first thought was: How does one "sleep off" a broken finger? That's what we always did when we were sick. I spiraled.

My younger sister and I were always together, with Mom, going somewhere, to a community event where we'd scavenge free food or tagging along to whichever gig my mother had at the time. She was poor. But she was also a musician and a fashion icon in our small corner of inner-city Houston. We hadn't always lived in such a big city. Port Arthur was home, then Fort Worth. But as Mom's dreams of music grew, she set her sights on Houston. It was all the same to me, places where we hopped from someone's couch or air mattress to another. Never our own rooms. Never a place we owned. But Mom was always there, full of smiles, warmth, and love. Though I wasn't sure how much smiling she would be doing when she arrived home and realized I'd hurt my finger and probably needed medical help.

I stuck it in ice and then butter before my little sister reminded me butter is for burns. But nothing I did to get it to stop hurting worked. When Mom walked in, my index finger was the size of a sausage. She sighed heavily and I could practically hear the words running through her mind by the slump in her shoulders. *Why is everything so hard for us all the time?* That was the first time I remember wondering that, too.

Two days later she picked me up from school early to take me to the doctor. I stood beside her as she checked me in. I hoped fiercely that this doctor's visit would be simple, easy—in and out. That whatever happened at that office wouldn't dull the usual gleam in Mom's eyes.

"Name and birthday?"

I told her and she jotted it down on her clipboard.

"And your insurance card?" She held out her hand, now looking at Mom, who smiled. But her smile didn't warm me up inside like it usually did. The creases that hugged around her eyes weren't a part of her real smile. They were lines that had been carved there a long time, deepening after a long night's work or when we'd get out of school with rumbling tummies. This smile wasn't happy. It was a mask. But I didn't know what insurance was at the time or why it made Mom look like she'd aged ten years in a single moment.

"I'll be paying out of pocket," I heard my mother say. And I remember it was like the clouds parted.

After the appointment, with my hand in a cast, we had to check out with the lady at the desk. And for a moment I wondered if Mom was telling the truth when she said she'd pay for it. Was she really going to pay for this cast thing? Or was there some way we could get out of here without doing that? Mom wasn't a liar though. She told me the truth, even if it was ugly. Like when she told me I did have a dad, and him not being around wasn't a bad thing. If she didn't want to give the full truth, she just wouldn't say anything at all. I watched with bated breath as her fingers unzipped her purse. When she pulled out a wad of cash, my mouth fell open.

"Go sit down over there, mammas," she told me, firmly. She smiled at the nurse, apologizing. For what I wasn't sure. I was still pinned in place by shock before I managed to drag myself over to the waiting area. How many side jobs did Mom have to work to get that much cash that quickly? Was that why the tired lines around her face seemed deeper than before? When my friends or my teachers got sick, they went to the doctor. They got medicine, if needed. It seemed so . . . simple. But nothing was simple when it came to my childhood and money. I didn't have to know precisely *how* she got all that money to know that it wasn't easy. In hindsight I realize it was only about $400. But again—I'd never seen that much money in my life, and it seemed like the layers of bills were reflected in the wrinkles in Mom's skin.

To eight-year-old me, the concept of poverty was like staring at my life through a fish-eye lens. It was all distorted by my vantage point. Mom was a really talented singer, among other day jobs—she worked *all* the time. But we avoided going to the doctor? I couldn't see the bigger picture. She was always working hard as if she was intending to build something lasting and meaningful for our family. But if we could hardly afford to even get my broken finger fixed, how could we afford to have any kind of life that looked like my friends'? How could Mom build anything when she had nothing to build from?

The next day I asked my teacher at school how much insurance costs.

"Baby, that's free," she said.

"Free?" I couldn't be hearing her right.

"Doesn't cost your family a dime."

So, it wasn't only money that could make things easier but certain schemes and plans? I wondered, *If insurance was free, why didn't we have it?*

━━━

Free. The word rang like a gong in my head as I lay down on Stacy's couch, trying to get comfortable for the night. As I rolled in my covers, pondering the shoddy state of my own fledgling business with the noise of the busy LA streets outside the window, everyone hustling and hurrying, I remembered that my mother only used the word "free" with genuine joy glazed in her eyes, once.

It was 2004 and I was in tenth grade. Mom picked me up from school in her red Jeep Cherokee. Rusted and well used, it made this funny sound when the air conditioning blew hard. And sometimes the inside handle would get stuck, but she was trusty and reliable.

And home. Literally.

I slid onto the seat beside my younger sister and tossed my backpack in the back on top of everything else we owned. All of it, stuffed in the trunk of a car.

"Where to, Mom?"

"Today"—she smiled, and it fluttered inside me like warm butterflies—"we're going to the Third Ward Spring Block Party festival."

My sister's face lit up, too. I buckled in as our "mobile home" zoomed off. That night we listened to live music and hung out with some of the influential faces on the Houston fashion scene. By the time we climbed back in the jeep that night, we were all tuckered out. I grabbed my winter coat from the back and stuffed it up under my head as Mom rolled around Houston to find a place for us to park to sleep. Some mornings I'd wake up to a beach, others some gorgeous vista where you could see the city landscape. But the next morning we woke up outside of a building I knew well—S.H.A.P.E.

S.H.A.P.E. is a community center dedicated to improving the lives of "people of African descent through programs and activities." It was a place where being Black was heralded. Every time I was there, I was steeped in affirmation of my culture and roots and how proud I should be of them. S.H.A.P.E. was a place of familiarity, where people talked like I talked, discussed things familiar to me, ate foods I recognized, played games I enjoyed. The coarse, coiled edges of their hair looked like the edges of mine; their bodies curved, swayed, and dipped just as mine did. They shopped at the stores where Mom and I shopped. S.H.A.P.E. was as much home as Mom's red jeep was. We went there a few times a week, especially on the weekends because they served free breakfast.

"You have a thing today and we can't go with you?" I asked.

"No. I have a surprise."

I sat up as she got out of the car, telling us to stay. I elbowed my sister awake. Mom came back to the car with a key. It was silver and round on the top and I remember my heart hiccupping in my chest.

We'd had many keys before. Keys to Mom's boyfriends' or friends' houses. Sometimes an aunt or something. The keys we were given always eventually had to be returned. The keys were never ours. But as Mom walked toward my sister and me, I noticed she held three identical copies. She handed me one. I swallowed. She gave my sister one, too. Then she stuck the other in her pocket. Her green eyes sparkled in a way I'd never seen before.

"Back in the car," she said, and we listened.

A hummingbird took flight in my chest as she drove through the neighborhood of Third Ward, around the community center, before parking in front of a house that was a replica of the others beside it. I eyed the house, wondering who it belonged to and why we needed to come over this early in the morning, my mind struggling to sew together the pieces of what was happening. It was a brownish-yellow brick home on a corner lot with a blotchy, half-dead front lawn. The door was different, I remember, because it had an arched frame and it reminded me of one of those magical doorways in stories we'd read as kids. The house's pointed eaves were also really tall, almost castle-like. It had small, square, shuttered windows. A tall chimney was right beside the front door alongside foggy panes of glass. It looked cozy. Goosebumps danced up my skin, but disbelief set my jaw. *What was this place? It couldn't be ours.*

We hustled out of the car and my mom gestured for me to put my key in the door first. It turned, and the door unlocked. Inside was a living room with a quaint kitchen made up of a fridge and stove with two narrow counters in between. The sink was beneath a window that looked at the neighbor's brick. An old wooden brown table was in the walkway wreathed in a pair of folding chairs. There was a couch in the living room, its leather peeling in places. And in the single bedroom there were two mattresses covered in white sheets with folded blankets on them.

"How much is all this, Mom?" I folded my arms, refusing to get excited about something that we'd just lose, again.

"It's *free*," she said with a look of total pride.

I steadied myself against the wall, my brow slashing downward in complete confusion. "You mean someone is just giving us a house?"

"*Sssh*, Ciera," my little sister said. "Mom said it's ours." I held up my hand to hush my sister so I could hear Mom's answer.

"That's exactly what I'm saying. Through S.H.A.P.E., I was able to connect with Project Row. This is completely free. No strings attached."

I pursed my lips. Still, I let my hands trail the ridges in the wall paint, imagining coming home here. The house wasn't new or perfect in any way. It had a short step up to it that would be easy to trip over if someone wasn't paying attention. The floors and counters were stained. But with evidence of cooking that took place there. Lots of cooking. *Happy memories.* My fingers traced crayon markings on the wall and the corner of my lip tugged up in a smile. I pictured kids and their mother standing over the stove, sitting at the table. The house also had a smattering of furniture, most a bit lumpy. My smile deepened at the rambunctious playtime that couch must have endured. The giggles these walls must have held.

"The family who used to live here just bought their own house. The lady's son just graduated high school."

This house had been well-loved by another family. A warmth nestled in my chest unfurled, no matter how hard my jaw ticked. It was intoxicating. It was hope.

Mom was trying to build something in our family and this free home was a foundational part of it. For the first time in my entire life, I sat down on a seat that I was sure would hold me for many years. We spent the rest of the morning setting up my half of my and my sister's room. I set out my chess championship medals on the floor. Six medals, six trophies for competing in chess at the state level as a kid. Me, one of only two Black kids in the entire competition and the only poor one, I bet. My best flex yet. Dust would cover them eventually. Maybe I'd let them collect dust for *years* if I wanted. I had a home. And it was free.

I've driven back by that house as an adult and I realized it had to be no more than 1,000 square feet, but to me it may as well have been a castle. Turning the knob every single time always felt like the first time. It sparkled with wonder and warmed with comfort.

Years later, sitting on my borrowed couch, as I thought back on breaking my finger and my teacher explaining to me that insurance to cover the medical bill should have been free for our family, I realized she'd meant Medicaid, free health insurance for low-income families. We were low income. We should have had insurance. But we didn't. That was a resource we didn't have, and it could have made life easier. It could have been a resource that we could build on. Maybe I would have played extracurricular sports regardless of the injury risk if keeping medical expenses minimal wasn't a concern. Maybe doing that could have exposed me to other passions and interests that I could have used later to fund college. I've never asked my mother why she didn't accept free insurance. The house was the only assistance my mother ever took. And it took her fourteen years of my life to decide to pursue that.

I lived in that free house from tenth grade until my second year of college and I was very grateful. But we had hopped around from one borrowed couch to the borrowed corner of a warehouse to the red jeep and on and on since I was in diapers. Remembering the incident with my finger, and the initial feeling of settling into our first steady home, I wondered what other free resources were out there that Mom hadn't taken advantage of. And *why*. Back then I was so grateful to have a mattress to sleep on that felt like my own, a door where I was sure the key would work, a home that didn't have wheels, that I never asked her.

As I lay on the couch, wrapped in my blanket, exhausted from the day's errands, trying to summon sleep, I was fully aware that my morning shift started in a few short hours. But all I could think about was how Mom struggled to build stability for us for *years*. When she finally took advantage of free resources, our entire lives changed. I could take the bus to school, Mom could use her money for food and other things with shelter taken care of. We could use our car as a car. We had a fridge, a stove, and a whole kitchen. I had neighbors, a community I became used to seeing every day. My life felt . . . different coming home to a home. Having that free house gave me stability I could then build upon.

I sat up, realizing that in this business predicament I found myself in, with limited resources, it felt like I was creating something with nothing like when I was a kid.

But that wasn't true.

I didn't have to build from nothing.

I could build by using everything I could get my hands on.

Just like my mom had when she pursued that free house.

Free stuff, donated stuff, favors from friends, borrowed things, grants, you name it. If it was something that I could acquire without spending money, it added to my repertoire of resources to build my business on. Those free resources could cement into a foundation I could stand on.

The number one reason most people don't start working toward their success goals is the misbelief that they need money (that they do not have) to get started. Have you ever heard some variation of *I want to start a podcast, but I can't afford a good mic* from someone who then proceeds to spend sixty dollars on a new pair of jeans they don't need? Or *I would love to start my own consulting firm and leave my nine-to-five eventually* from someone who looks at their current company's multimillion-dollar operation, their public-facing messaging online, and concludes there's no way they could create something that grand, not realizing all it takes is starting with one client who believes in the value they offer and building from there. Or maybe you've heard *I really want to meal plan and cook balanced meals instead of eating fast food every day, but I can't afford to spend extra money on good Tupperware, and I don't want those expensive vegetables to go to waste. I'll just cut calories where I can instead.* This person might proceed to order a Diet Coke in lieu of a regular Coke, setting aside her goal of changing her eating habits yet again. The point isn't that she likes her burger meal with a Coke. There is no shame to my fellow burger-loving hotties. (Shout-out to the no spread, mustard, mayo with grilled onions and light chilis In-N-Out burger.) It's that she's setting aside what's important to her because she *thinks* she doesn't have the money to act on her goals with seriousness. And that's just not true.

Whether it's because we aren't recognizing that we have the

power to change our habits, or we choose the easy path rather than going after what we really want (which is almost always harder), so many of us focus on what we *don't* have, creating an obstacle for ourselves and then shutting down, rather than focusing on what we *do* have and *can* do, which is almost always more than we realize!

As well as "I don't have the money," the other common excuse I hear is from my mom circles about how they would start working out but joining a gym with the cost of childcare just isn't doable. Girl, if you can't afford it, pull out your yoga mat in your living room. Or pop that baby in the stroller and walk three miles. Or take them to the playground and run *around* the play structure to get those steps in. (Shout-out to my friend Jess who actually did this when her kids were little. I'm not sure I'd be this motivated, to be honest.)

In the professional sector, Small Business Trends reports that one of the top reasons aspiring entrepreneurs never take the plunge and start a business is because of a belief that they don't have the money. It's a well-known fact that most businesses fail in their first five years because of lack of "working capital," or cash flow. So many of us aspiring entrepreneurs clam up at statistics like that and erect stifling obstacles. These perspectives are 100 percent reality. Childcare for a mom who needs to work out is a real need. Rewiring our routine to eat healthy with ease and convenience is a whole process. And starting a new business comes with a lot of financial pressure for cash flow. But that doesn't mean don't start a business, don't work out, don't eat healthy. It means find a way to get started that doesn't cost a bunch of money. There are always ways to do what you want, get support, or find resources you need on the cheap, you just need to get inventive.

Fully wrapping my mind around this strategy sent a jolt buzzing though my insides. My heart sped up in excitement as I sat there mulling all this over. Socioeconomically, I was on the outside of my counterparts in Los Angeles. But growing up poor, on the outside, I knew better than anyone the value of free resources and that sometimes finding them meant hunting for them.

Project Row had been an option for my mother *long* before we ever took advantage of it. I would not do that. I would not wait to take advantage of things *right* at my fingertips. I didn't choose to come into this world without a cradle of inherited generational resources to fall back on. Neither did Mom or her mother. Or their slave ancestors before them. But right then, in 2012, sitting on that couch with the pieces of a business in the making in plastic grocery sacks all around me, my insides twinged with a glimmer of gratitude at a childhood that pushed me to the margins. I knew exactly what I had to do next.

I set my mind to getting my hands on as many free resources as I could. I immediately dove into research, carving out time in my already jam-packed schedule. I perused government website after government website, looking for any sort of resources for Black entrepreneurial business owners. I did exhaustive research on retail selling platforms for people who didn't have any money into the wee hours of the night for days. I researched between thrifting trips and selling more on Instagram. Sometimes searching sites like these felt like being on a hamster wheel. Often, the information was convoluted and not easy to sift through to find explicit, action-able details. But I persisted. If there was a way that I could reshape my business to increase my productivity for free, I was going to find it. I'm like a dog with a bone when I'm determined.

Several days later, I found something—a site called Big Cartel, which allowed me to list five items for sale completely free. The site also collected the customer's information, provided a secure platform to take their payment, and kept some kind of accounting records for me. Goodbye IG comments and PayPal links. I had something much more efficient and professional now. Customers could even leave notes for me at checkout, which was really help-ful for sharing size specifications.

After work the next day, I followed my usual routine and listed five thrifted outfits on my new shopping site. All five outfits sold the same day. Switching to Big Cartel wasn't the only part of my business that needed a professional refresh. But it was a start. I also invested in professional editing software, a rolling rack to hold my clothes, and an inexpensive starter digital camera.

You don't need much to build success if you have imagination and determination.

What I realize now is that when you're trying to build something—a business, a stable foundation for your family, or something else—it often feels like you're building from nothing. This is a debilitating lie. You are building from *anything* you can get your hands on. Your resources are not just those you inherit or have earned. Before you finish the sentence "I don't have . . ." stop glar-ing at your empty wallet and *expand* your pot of resources. Re-search government programs, look into specific opportunities for financial support or any type of resources that cater to your marginalization or special interest groups that suit you. There are a whole host of women-focused organizations itching to empower and support self-motivated people like us.

Whether you want to go back to school while working, snag the senior position at your company, or raise funds for a new building in your community, switch how you think about what you don't have in order to meet your goal. Start focusing on what is available to you if you look a little further afield.

And watch the world open up to you.

By month's end, that's exactly what happened to me. I paid my half of the rent on time, and it felt so good. That experience taught me two undeniable truths about myself. One: I have plenty to build from. And two: I am unstoppable.

THE OUTSIDE SCOOP

I Examined the Relationship I Had with Money Growing Up

On Saturdays as a kid, we would choose to go to community events where there would be food available. Instead of breaking a ten-dollar bill we might have on hand to grab fast food, we'd choose the free option every time.

Then, my clothes were rarely new, if ever. I always looked as if I had styled myself with gently used hand-me-downs. (Because I basically had!) But we had no other option. And I hated that. Eventually, I began to make my own money with side jobs as a teenager and found it very hard to part with it. Suddenly, I had more options. But I trusted only the option that was most familiar to me—cheap or free. I learned at a very early age that earning money takes a lot of effort for someone like me who is an outsider socio-economically, and there is no guarantee that when I spend money I'll get more to replace it.

Fast-forward to landing in LA. Girl, I never visualized myself as a *business owner*. Are you kidding me? No way. Ciera who knew how to stretch a twenty-dollar bill for two weeks couldn't afford to step out on a limb and build a million-dollar fashion brand. (Joke's on me, I guess!) Even then, my ability to imagine a future for myself was limited to risk-averse, practical options that were safe choices. I couldn't *afford* to make plans based on my passions! That was a privilege outsiders in my shoes didn't get.

But this is a lie!

The truth is that I hadn't considered *how* I could build a business on zero dollars. I mean even that suggestion sounds a bit unhinged as you read it. But when I reflected on my relationship with money as a kid, I realized how useful that experience could be in shifting my paradigm and building success in my future.

The simple truth is not everything has to cost money. I knew this well, but I'd subconsciously buried the traumatizing tidbits of growing up poor and risked smothering all the gems with it. Hearing the whisper of that poor child in my ear reminding me that there could be a free option was a good thing. I'd shut out that voice because I didn't want to dwell on my own trauma. But it was and still is helpful for me to tune in to that voice every so often—to remember, recognize, and sit with just how poor I was as a kid so that poor Ciera's way of thinking could be used positively.

When I realized this, my mind opened up. I could *become* a business owner if I could make things, use the resources of others, ask a friend, or negotiate for a bargain.

Perhaps your relationship and history with money are nothing like mine were. Maybe money was present in abundance and because of that you've taken it for granted. Consider diving deep into the ways your relationship with money *was* helpful and ways it *was not*. The key is to realize that whatever your relationship was is foundational in how you view financial obstacles to your future success today. What relationship did you have with money growing up, good or bad? How has it shaped your perspective on how equipped you are to start working toward your goals? What stories do you tell yourself about money that need to be updated or erased?

I Used My Time Instead of My Money

At the start, my business needed me, not money. An influx of cash would have been great, but as we've established, I didn't have that. What I did have was time. Instead of looking for ways to spend money to make my business run more efficiently, in those early days of Babes I looked for ways to expend more *time* to avoid denting my wallet. I hand sewed instead of hiring a tailor, I would visit a public work center where they had community sewing machines and use those instead of buying one. This meant longer days, less sleep—but in those early days, it was more important to me that I spent my time rather than the money that was actually starting to flow quite nicely.

I was shocked by how much money could be offset by expending more time. At a certain point, when I started to bring in a little more income, this was inefficient, but in the early stages of business, I wasn't focused on efficiency—I was focused on effectiveness. I wanted to establish something that I could build on. I knew once I'd built something sustainable that had proven it worked over a certain period of time, I could pivot later to focus on efficiency. Because let's be super honest, working myself to death doesn't sound like a fun success journey to be on. I paid my dues up front so that I could literally pay my dues (bills) later, ha ha. I trusted that I would instinctually know when it was time to make a change. For Babes, that time came much sooner than I expected.

Think, are there resources you can you substitute for an abundance of money? How might they propel you quicker toward accomplishing your goals?

3

Build from the Inside Out

AFFIRMATION

I will be me

I have a big butt.

I grew up in an era when big butts were hidden with narrow-tailored clothes. But I learned very early to embrace my booty. So when I was getting dressed for my first LA party, I knew whatever I wore, it should at least make my butt look good. It was two months after I'd met my roommate's ultimatum and I received my first invite to a *real* Hollywood party. The thrifted outfits I posted on Big Cartel were selling out almost immediately at this point. I kept it to the five free items plan because between my part-time job and thrifting, I was able to save *just* enough to make rent each month and thrift a few outfits. But there was no buffer. My margins were like jeans that only zipped when you sucked your breath in. Still, technically, my business was a business even if I didn't feel like I'd arrived yet. So when I got the invitation to the premiere for a documentary Spike Lee had produced, I decided to take a night off and just have a good time.

This was my first real party in LA. I didn't have any trendy LA street wear. There were no designer labels in my closet either. There was no time or extra cash to make another trip to the resale shop to thrift something new. I flipped through my closet backward and forward. That night, I was going to have to wear a tried-and-true Ciera Rogers vintage look.

I pulled out a dress made of a cotton material. When I slipped it on and felt the way it hugged around me in all the right places, I remembered how much I loved it. It was a frumpy patterned dress that was probably someone's grandmother's nightgown when I bought it. But I cinched the back so that it hugged at the waist and was loose on my shoulders. I trimmed the bottom so it was jagged and showed a bit of thigh. It was casual, but nice, and had a "tailored" fit. I threw on a long sweater over my arms and a crossbody bag, and slipped on a pair of open-toe shoes to finish the look. I looked cute.

The premiere was held at the W hotel and was full of celebs, which isn't unusual for LA, but was still unusual to me! The first celeb I ever saw was Rihanna at a bowling alley, and when I spotted her, I couldn't move. No one really reacted to seeing them, usually treating them like regular people, so I tried hard to do the same. But I couldn't help myself. Inside this party, my heart skipped a beat each time I spotted someone famous. I grabbed a drink from a passing tray and held on to it tight as my eyes roved the audience for familiar faces.

My hands went clammy. The friend I'd attended with was much more comfortable than I was. I stuck to her side like a fly. Everything was *so* nice. To be clear, this wasn't a formal event. People were not wearing ball gowns or tuxedos. But they may as well have been. To me everything and everyone oozed success. The way people carried themselves, how they spoke about their latest trips or some swanky gala they had coming up, and also the way they dressed—the effortless style that I knew, because I knew fashion—dripped with dollar signs. No one in the crowd had on the same outfit, technically. They dressed differently and yet all the same. Their clothes said *rich, money, status*. I suddenly and quite desperately wanted to blend in. After all, I was in LA to build something successful, something stable, something life-changing *big*.

The woman standing behind me, waiting to get to the aisle where her seat was, caught my eye. She was wearing a black fitted dress, which stuck out to me because it couldn't be more basic. It didn't have any colorful stitching or embellishments. It didn't even have an interesting neckline. But the *fabric*. It was the kind of dress that doesn't stretch. It curved around her body flawlessly. The dress looked as if it was handmade with the finest material specially for her. Gold rings hugged her knuckles and what I assume were real diamonds sparkled in her ears. She was model-tall but wore black Louboutin heels, and her hair was swept back in a chic bun. Then there was me beside her. I suddenly felt like a chunky toddler with a costume on from Walmart. The same dress I'd loved moments before now felt like a neon flashing sign saying FRAUD. I was an outsider at that party in every possible way.

The woman sat down in her row closer to the front, and my friend and I found our seats in the back.

"I belong here," I whispered to myself. As I sat in my seat, I kept my head up, avoiding eye contact with anyone. But my head swiveled in every direction regardless of how hard I tried to stop it. I pulled my sweater around me tightly, covering the roughly sewn edges of my DIY dress. Then the lights lowered for the movie, and I exhaled.

In the darkness, with no one watching, I sunk in my seat more comfortably and let a smile tease my lips. I was at a freaking premiere for Spike Lee! At the same time, the shock nudged me with unease. I was comfortable showing up to that party as myself—being myself—*before* I got there and saw everyone else there. I'd told myself I belonged there. Now that I'd seen how much of an outsider I was, did I really believe that? Nausea swirled in my gut in answer to that question, killing my smile.

And for the first half of the film, my mind was somewhere else entirely.

I was thirteen, in middle school, and starting a new school *again*. An unavoidable symptom of moving from place to place as a kid meant changing schools *a lot*. I attended a different elementary school every year. And in the three years of middle school, I changed schools twice. I was well accustomed to showing up somewhere new. I had a whole strategy. I'd find someone I admired, become their friend, and the new place wouldn't feel so isolating.

Our friendship usually consisted of my looking up to the way they dressed, wore their hair, carried themselves. Eventually I'd find I'd adopted some of their mannerisms, some of their turns of phrase, and on occasion, when I could, I started to dress like them. But this time, showing up at Gregory-Lincoln middle school was altogether different, because it was the middle of the school year and the first group of girls I befriended were super popular, trendily dressed *cheerleaders*.

I can still feel the way bumps danced up my skin as I entered the cafeteria with a tray of pizza and chocolate milk in my hand. That morning when we'd woken up, I'd checked the ice cooler in the art warehouse where we were living. Mom had a friend who was an artist. He rented a large warehouse, and he carved out a corner of it for the air mattress where my sister and I slept. But it was a place of work, not a home, so it didn't have a refrigerator or anything like that. Still, we kept a cooler and Mom usually put things in there. This morning it had slim pickings, so I was extra excited to devour lunch at school.

I scanned the cafeteria for a place to land. Everyone was already absorbed in their own conversations. The social order had already gelled. My grip tightened on my tray.

"Over here," the counselor who'd shown me to my classes that morning said. "This is Stephanie. Stephanie, meet Ciera."

Stephanie wore her hair in a donut bun. Tendrils hung from the edges near her ears and her temple. She wore a fitted preppy-girl sweater over her uniform, which had been expertly ironed. Her nails were evenly trimmed and polished without any chips. She was neat, tidy, and well put together. *She was perfect.* I stood straighter, my gaze falling to my own wrinkled khaki skirt. (Living in the corner of the warehouse also meant pulling my clothes out of one of those disposable plastic drawers.) I didn't even know this girl, but I wanted to impress her. As her eyes traced me up and down, I smoothed my clothes the best I could and angled my tray so she couldn't see my fraying-edge tennis shoes. The thought of my unkempt hair from waking up in a frenzy rolled through my mind like a tumbleweed.

My stomach churned, but somehow hunger seemed so insignificant in that moment. Stephanie pursed her lips. I followed her to her table where the other cheerleaders were hanging out. They were all poised and put together like Stephanie. I'd never felt like more of an outsider among a group of girls my age in my entire life. They asked if I'd cheered before and I told them no. I sat and kept quiet, studying their every move.

"Can I have your chocolate milk, Tia?" Stephanie asked.

Tia swapped her. And a few others did the same, too. Apparently this was a ritual, swapping parts of lunch that they didn't want.

"You can have mine, too," I cut in, watching for smile lines around their eyes. "I don't like chocolate milk." *I loved chocolate milk.* I tossed mine in the mix and plucked a fry from my tray. The other girls weren't touching the other things on their tray. Only the fries. I grabbed another handful.

"Those your real eyes?" Tia asked.

"Yeah," I said, gnawing my lip timidly. "You have pretty long lashes." I reciprocated the compliment.

"You think?" Tia flipped her hair.

"Oh lord, don't give Tia any more reason to think she's all that," Stephanie teased. Tia's pursed lips split in a knowing grin before she and Steph slapped hands. The whole group of girls laughed. Tia stood up from the table and strutted up and down the cafeteria, pretending to model.

"Thanks, girl," she said to me, her friends still chuckling dotingly when this weird sound suddenly erupted from my throat. It was high-pitched and kind of sounded like a pig dying an excruciating death. It was a giggle. I . . . was laughing in a much higher tone than usual. Like they were. It felt weird, like wearing shoes on the wrong feet. But I was determined to blend in and be more like them. And less like me.

The cheerleader crew and I spent the rest of lunch together and even played four square at recess, which was like an unspoken pact of ride-or-die friendship. The next day I slicked my hair back and put a sweater over my school shirt. It wasn't the kind with small buttons and fur along the sleeves, which was all the rage then, but it was the vibe. The best I could do anyway. I turned, admiring myself. This was the *style*. This was what the girls who'd accepted me into their friend group wore. These were girls who moved through the school with confidence and poise. These girls looked like they had it together. I wanted to have it together. Or at least look like I did. Instead of strutting around carefree as they did, I was consumed with worry about the soles coming off my shoes. Maybe if I moved like them, I'd feel like them. And who knows, maybe one day I could *be* like them.

Looking back on that time, I realize more than anything I wanted to be anyone else but myself.

Those girls and I stayed besties through the end of middle school. When it was time to go to high school, I was sad to start a new school with new faces. But the next time it was less than forty-eight hours on campus before I spotted a junior in the hall-way eyeing me. She was dressed to the nines . . . well, as much as one could in a uniform. Her clothes were pressed, hair neat. Her posture was really impressive, and she moved like she knew who she was. I stared for so long that by the time I blinked, she was right in front of me.

"Hi," she said. "Are you a freshman?"

I thought of Stephanie again, how cool she was. How she and the cheerleaders became my people. This girl was my shot to do that here in high school.

"Hi, I am, yes. My name is Ciera."

She nodded. "I'm Jess. If you need anything, let me know. And there's a social club meeting at lunch this week. You should come."

She walked off and I collapsed against my locker in relief. I'd found a friend *and* someone to emulate. Someone to look up to. Someone to show me how I should move and who I should be. I wish I could say this habit died a horrible death after high school. But, alas, it did not. When I first set foot on the University of Houston campus, I ran into a gorgeous girl with velvety, flawless, deep-brown skin. Her hair curled effortlessly. Her jeans and off-the-shoulder top were simple and yet so chic. I didn't say anything the first time I saw her. But after my first couple classes, I saw her again in the restroom. By now I knew how this went. I was well practiced at looking outside myself for someone to be like. Her name was Britney, and we're still friends to this day.

——

As I pressed myself back into the seat of the movie premiere, ruminating on my teenage attempts to fit in, I studied the shapes of the bodies in the audience. There was no emulating them in style. I couldn't afford it. I didn't live in the posh parts of town or hang at the places they frequented. I didn't even eat at the places they ate. I could not actually tailor my clothes or look so effortlessly accomplished. Inside, I knew who I was, but outside is what they saw. And there was only so much pretending I could do.

"Are you all right?" my friend asked, and I realized my nails were dug into the arm of the seat. I told her I was fine because admitting that I wasn't out loud would only make it more real. Tia, Stephanie, Jessica, Britney. The list was long. I didn't have that here. And I couldn't thrift my way into it either. I was different from everyone in this room, which felt like everyone in the successful circles in this entire city.

I had no choice but to be me. To be the outsider.

And in that moment, that terrified me.

My stomach sloshed as the lights came up. The crowd shuffled out of their seats toward a reception that was just starting. My friend and I refreshed our drinks, and I was determined to shrug off the insecurity trying to drape itself around my shoulders. I caught a glimpse of myself in a huge decorative mirror as we passed.

"I belong here," I whispered to myself again and chugged my champagne, when a short man with sharp eyebrows hurried in my direction.

"Oh my God, Spike Lee is walking toward us." I pinched my friend and put my back to the wall, tugging on my sweater, smoothing my clothes. He'd been circling the room in and out of conversations. My friend snagged an invite to this party from a friend of a friend. She didn't know Spike. Neither of us did! She was just as shocked.

When he reached us, and didn't recognize us, he offered his hand. "I'm Spike, and you are?"

"Ciera."

He greeted us both and for a moment I forgot to breathe. I was talking to Spike Lee, *the* Black filmmaker, director, screenwriter, and actor who was responsible for producing some of the most impactful stories in history to center Black characters. My heart stuttered in my chest. He was looking at me expectantly as if he'd just asked a question.

"Sorry, what did you say?"

"I asked what you do?"

He's asking who I am. My gaze flicked to the lady in the fine black dress, and I straightened and held my shoulders back, holding the stem of my champagne flute more daintily, with loose fingers, the way others did. But despite how I mimicked the air of belonging, his question sparked dozens of images popping up in my mind. A rusted red jeep. Fraying tennis shoes. No amount of manners and proper posture could erase the culmination of events that led me to standing in that ballroom in those thrifted clothes with a poorly glued-in, frizzy hair weave. What did I do? Who was I?

As I swirled the champagne in my glass, I thought about the first outfit I sold on Instagram. Then it shifted to Stacy's expression when I handed her that first month's rent. The late nights of sewing, the fact that I "designed" everything I was wearing. The persistent SOLD OUT blue button on Big Cartel. The comments on my social media posts heralding my clothes for being "unique," "unlike anything in stores." That one-of-a-kind vibe was the same style that I was armored in standing in front of Spike Lee.

I didn't blend in. And that was a good thing, I realized.

I stand out when I choose to be myself.

And standing out can lend itself to success-birthing opportunities.

I stopped swishing my glass and met Spike's eye. He still stared patiently, and what was probably no more than ten awkward seconds felt like a week as I relived the journey I'd been on in LA. The nothing I'd started with and the something I was becoming.

"I'm a stylist and fashion designer," I said. The words tasted unfamiliar on my tongue, but I said them like I meant them. I spent a few minutes telling him about my novel approach to selling clothes.

"I see," he said, eyeing my current outfit. "So, you made this?"

"I did."

He pinched his chin. "Do you have a website with your styling work?"

I shook my head no. I only had Big Cartel, a shopping landing page, which at the moment was sold out.

"If you don't have a website, you won't be taken seriously." He handed me his card. "Once you get your stuff ironed out, shoot me an email. I'd like to check it out. Nice to meet you both." He walked away and I froze. Stunned. Someone influential in Hollywood was interested in my thrifted fashion designing.

That night I tossed and turned, replaying Spike's words in my head. That day I was tugged back to my formative habit of emulating others, and I reflected on the initial discomfort I felt at the movie premiere being myself. An unsettling question stabbed me in the ribs. Here I was hustling hard to create a clothing brand that's all about thinking outside the box, being distinct, fresh, and authentic to my customers' bodies. Leaning into outsiderness. But how could I bring this concept of authenticity to its ripest fruition in my business if I was not authentic with myself first?

At this premiere, I struggled. It's like my clothes were shouting, *I'm comfortable being me no matter what.* When in reality I was still looking outside of myself for some signal of who I should be. The truth slapped me so hard I had to get out of bed, pull my bonnet off, and stare at myself in the mirror again. I had to look at the girl who was so determined to look elsewhere. That party was a fortunate wake-up call.

A reminder to *be* the person inside that I was dressing like on the outside.

I would be myself. Full stop.

I wish I could say after that party I never struggled with my identity or looking outside of myself for signals of who I should be ever again. The truth is it took me years from college into adulthood to break the cycle of focusing on the ways others seemed to have it all together and instead focus on myself. It required a lot of intentional reflecting, affirming the things I love about myself *and* the things I wanted to improve. To rid myself of that bad habit, I had to replace it with a new one—thinking about myself differently. Self-love is too cute of a term to describe what I had to do. It felt more like peeling my skin off, layer by layer, exposing my raw self and falling in love with the blood and guts underneath. I love my cellulite, the way my sides dip and curve. I love the inner-city poorer areas where I grew up. I love knowing what it's like to have a ketchup sandwich for dinner. It's nostalgic and galvanizing. It's me.

And my company was born as an extension of all I'd experienced growing up. These days, when I feel the tendency to look outside myself creep up, I know what to do. I'm aware of the indications that I may be losing touch with the Ciera *I* want to be. Who I want to be can (and should) evolve over time. But on my terms, not because of a false perception of worth that I ascribe to others and deny myself. Actively choosing to fully exist in my own skin means listening to my own reasoning, allowing my own perspective to have authority over how I view myself. Doing that is powerfully transformative because it dislodges damaging internalized ideas about who I am allowed to be.

I have to be me.

I want to be.

After the premiere, I decided to make the message of loving ourselves more explicit and central to my business. Looking in the mirror, I realized that every woman, in every size and shape, at every stage of life—because our bodies change *a lot*—should feel secure and confident in their own skin. For the first time, I saw and accepted myself, my shape, my experiences, my changing form, and I wanted to make other women feel that way. I knew if I wanted to really inspire women to wholly love themselves and feel comfortable in their own skin, it had to start with me. To capture the spirit of self-acceptance and celebration, I picked the name Babes and Felines for my company, but eventually shortened it to Babes.

Being an outsider at that party ignited something in me. It was the wake-up call I needed. Do not miss your wake-up call.

There's a box where everyone else is. Get out of it. Be different.

Be *you*. When you are unapologetically and authentically your-self, you set yourself apart, which not only helps you stand out but also emboldens you to be confidently aware of who you are. Grab hold of this powerful self-reckoning to make your work stand out, in whatever industry, whether breaking in, starting something, or moving up. You do not have to parent the way your friends do or the way your parents did. Your life's components, the routine of your day, the house rules don't have to be organized the same way as your nosy neighbor who seems to have it all together. (She doesn't, I promise you.) Whether professional or personal, there is only *one* you. Pull together your experiences, sift through the tap-estry of who you are and why, and execute your game plan with a strategy and style only *you* can create. Then use that new secure sense of self to transform whatever you're working on from the inside out. Or, as in my case, recognize that you've done that in your work life, and then do it on yourself.

THE OUTSIDE SCOOP

I Decided to Stand Out for What I Stand For

I liked the way I dressed even if it wasn't expensive or on trend. Who decided trends anyway? What if I wanted to start a new trend? As ideas whirred in my brain about my thrifted style of dress in a city that could chew me up and spit me out, I realized I dressed the way I dressed because it made me feel comfortable and confident. I decided to lean in harder to this idea and be even more intentional about making sure that my style of dress made me feel good because of the way it hugged my hips and waist and complemented my eyes. I became fairly obsessed with defining my own personal style and really thinking about each clothing purchase decision, weighing why I wanted it. Did I believe it was objectively cute? Or did having it make me feel worthy in ways I hadn't before? As I continued to refine my style choices and hold myself accountable in the mirror each day, I realized that I was inadvertently standing up for girls shaped like me. Saying it's okay to dress in a way that isn't typical because my clothes fit my curvy body better. Babes grew more and more defined by this philosophy. This not fitting in and curating a style to my curvy figure became the soapbox around which I built my entire company. And it thrives, I believe, in part because I stand for its mission so boldly. Which begs the question: What are you fiercely passionate about? How does it seep into your work? Can you lean into it harder? How would your work change if you opened the floodgates on your passions, letting them transform what you do every day?

4

Invest in Worthy Relationships

AFFIRMATION

I am deserving of the very best in life

'm not saying the world would be better off without men. But I'm not *not* saying that.

I used to have the worst luck with them, which is why when I arrived at Red O ten minutes before a dinner reservation *without* my boyfriend, I was relieved. I had one goal for that night—be memorable. I was dining with my friend Ranna and some others on the entrepreneur scene in LA and I was determined to make a good impression. No more being starstruck, not being able to think of words. I was a fashion designer in LA with a whole-ass website. It was 2013, an entire year after that first Hollywood party, and Spike's words *still* played like a resounding drum in my head. I'd even expanded on his advice and made my business look and feel more professional overall by getting a nicer camera with lenses I could swap out, professional light boxes to really level up the quality of my photos, and cute Babes-branded packaging. I even built a photography studio in my home office (yes, I had a proper office!), so I could do shoots there if I wanted. I was weaning off of thrifted looks and beginning to sell looks that I designed. Babes was my only job now. It was the real deal. I certainly felt more official and the extra zeros in my bank account echoed that sentiment. I had even moved off Stacy's couch into a two-bedroom apartment with my sister. Ciera Rogers was on her way.

Ranna and her friends were already seated when I found their table at the restaurant. The back of my neck broke out in sweat as I strutted confidently in their direction. I wasn't late. They were just super early. Half of the benefit of networking and meeting people is to make a lasting impression. But arriving last to the table wasn't my idea of a good start. I shook hands with everyone, noting that an order of drinks had already gone around. I slid into my chair and sipped untouched water.

As I jumped into small talk my phone buzzed.

I squeezed the side button to silence it just as the conversation moved in my direction.

"How did you get into fashion, Ciera? Is that what you've always done or—?" The question came from Helen, a successful boutique owner who had a clothing store on Melrose Avenue. My phone buzzed again. It was my boyfriend, Ken. My stomach sloshed. I picked at the hem of my shirt. "Sorry, what was the question?"

I felt like an idiot stumbling over my words. I was pretty confident around new people at this point. But I was babbling like someone who didn't know how to have a conversation. My hand squeezed around my phone, which was now lighting up and buzzing nonstop. I slipped my phone beneath the table into my lap. I wanted to bury it in my purse but didn't want to risk not knowing if he called again.

"I asked about fashion," Ranna's friend said as the server took orders. "How'd you get into it?"

I blew out a breath. I hated feeling nervous. I worked hard, I wanted to believe I deserved this outing. I wanted to believe I deserved a lot of things. I'd be doing just fine if my phone would just stop—

Buzz. Buzz. Buzz.

I sighed. "Sorry, do you mind if I just . . ." I tapped my phone and answered. His face appeared. It was a FaceTime call. "I'm at dinner with Ranna," I said before he could get a word in.

"Where you at? You're supposed to call when you get there."

Eyes darted around the table. Silence.

"Who's all there? Let me see."

This was our routine. When I arrived anywhere, I was supposed to FaceTime him and let him see who I was with and where I was—whether it was dinner with friends or Whole Foods. He was either coming along with me or watching from across the screen. The most shocking part in all of this is that getting into a relationship with someone like Ken was a slippery slope. He didn't show me these behaviors in the beginning. And as I grew more attached to him emotionally, I began to passively excuse names he'd call me or expectations he'd set, such as calling him everywhere I went. Or allowing him to tag along anytime I went anywhere. I didn't realize all of that was a giant red flag that he was incredibly insecure.

The table said hello to Ken and didn't make much of the situation, but I was mortified. Not because this was new. But just because I'd hoped I could get there ahead of everyone, show Ken that I was with my one friend he approved of, and then hang up and enjoy my meet and greet. There was more than one benefit to showing up early that night.

When the evening ended and everyone left, I just sat at the table ruing how embarrassed I still felt, wondering, *Why do I put up with this?* Just posing the question made my insides twist. Ken had called a dozen more times and I kept promising him I'd be home really soon. But I was still pinned to my seat trying to figure out this power he had over me. I wondered, *What do I deserve?* Judging by what I put up with—not much. The more I stewed, the more my thoughts wandered to my first relationship with a man—my father.

It was time for a real drink.

I was almost fourteen when I met my dad properly for the first time. Mom had wrangled my sister and me in the car after school, and I remember the way I sank into the comfort of the back-seat cushions. I slipped off my shoes and stretched my toes. Then she said, "We're going to James Coney Island." I couldn't believe my ears. We were going to eat at this local hot dog joint, and I couldn't have been more excited. The only way she could have topped this was if she'd said we were going to get Pappadeaux or something. Or to a shoe store. But food was, and maybe still is, my favorite thing. So I was on cloud nine.

The car pulled to a stop in the parking lot, and I remember the way Mom's expression changed. She was styled beautifully, as usual, but it was her eyes that read differently. And the way she shifted ever so slightly in her seat. A sudden tightness cinched in her shoulders, and I felt my own back tense. Then she sighed.

"What?" I asked, trying to seem unbothered.

"We're meeting someone here."

Someone. If it was a friend, she would have said their name. Those two syllables, some-one, carried the weight of fear, worry, hope, and something else in Mom I couldn't quite place.

"Who?" I insisted. Her eyes flicked to my sister, who smiled. My mom was always calm under pressure, smiling, happy, full of light. But in that moment, I wondered what made her shoulders sag as if she was suddenly completely exhausted.

"Your sister got in touch with some relatives who located your dad. Richard is his name."

I dug my nails into the seat, my appetite gone. She opened my door, and I lugged my legs, which now felt like lead, one by one out of the car. I didn't care to meet Richard. I couldn't remember ever meeting him and I'd been fine with that. Mom never prevented him from getting in contact with us. His not reaching out to be a dad was his choice. So I'd pushed the concept of a dad out of my brain. I buried it in a box in the crevices of my mind, nailed it shut, and locked it in a closet. I didn't have a dad. I had a mom. That was enough. But meeting him meant he was real. That there was a closet full of things I hadn't sorted through. It meant he knew about me and decided I wasn't worth the love a dad is supposed to give a daughter. It meant, in his eyes, I didn't deserve the unconditional love, support, and time of a father. I didn't have words for this at the time. I just knew I didn't want to eat hot dogs anymore.

Mom led us inside and I spotted Richard immediately. He had my same nose, my hairy arms, the same heart-shaped head and full lips. It was like staring in a mirror at a reflection I never knew existed. I wanted to smash the mirror. Not sit down and have a meal in front of it.

We ordered food and I watched as he let Mom pay. My jaw ticked. *Worthless*, I thought to myself. When we sat down, he poked and prodded me with questions, and I could hardly hear the words out of his mouth. Instead of listening, I was watching how different Mom was now from in the car. She seemed perfectly fine suddenly, which baffled me. How could she sit there and not be annoyed? Her hands lay leisurely in her lap. She was as poised as ever. But Mom was well practiced at putting forth what she wanted the world to see. Amid our shelter and food insecurity she built an entire reputation for styling and throwing swanky events. So perhaps this was another mask she was wearing to keep us together.

"She looks so much like me, Nancy," he said to my mom, and I flinched at the use of a name she'd left behind when we fled Port Arthur, where she'd met him. Mom was Zoe now. Didn't he know that? He did. He must not care, I thought, and he somehow became even worse in my mind.

"He asked you a question." My little sister elbowed me. She had hungered for this meeting. I didn't know what to say, so I didn't say anything. The conversation moved on and Richard's eyes flicked to me magnetically every few minutes. My sister was embroiled in the chatter. But all I could do was pick apart everything about his physique that reminded me of myself. It made me sick. I didn't take a single bite of my food. I was waiting for something of substance to come out, like an explanation for where he'd been. Or an apology for being absent. But the only words he actually said were more of the same, complimenting my appearance, noting how much I look like him. Before we left, he wrapped his arms around me in a hug and I turned into a statue, just holding my breath waiting for it to be over.

My father hadn't shown interest in claiming me as a kid, in being an actual father. So whatever he wanted from me at that point, I wasn't open to it. After meeting him, I realized I'd dodged a bullet. Still, I couldn't lie to myself and pretend that some part of me didn't wish my father had made different choices in those thirteen years. That he'd taken his contribution to my genetic composition more seriously. That he'd partnered with my mother so she didn't have to struggle so hard to provide for us.

That hunger to be claimed by him wasn't something I was always conscious of. But thanks to Ken's embarrassing intrusion at dinner and a nice splash of vodka, I was sucked into reflecting on my dating history. And it was glaringly apparent that my nonexistent relationship with Richard had left its mark on me.

As I stared at my ninth missed phone call from Ken in that restaurant, I could no longer ignore the truth of why I put up with all his bullshit. It hit me like a ton of bricks—Ken was the first partner to give me what my father, for thirteen years, refused to.

Before Ken, I'd gone through years of being interested in guys who weren't interested in any sort of formal relationship status with me. They liked me, but never enough, I guess, to want to formally title me girlfriend. I didn't deserve that level of commitment in their eyes. And that annoyed me for reasons I didn't have words for then. Their not claiming me didn't stop me from emotionally investing in them and getting hurt. There was a security,

I imagined, when the person you care about is willing to proclaim to the world that you belong to each other. I hungered for that. And Ken was the first partner to give that to me.

When I suggested a relationship to Ken, he didn't flinch. I felt valued and wanted and loved. That lie blinded me the entire year and a half we were together. I convinced myself that the way he treated me was real love. And the way I accommodated his desire to control my every move was patient love, selfless love. I even argued to myself once that since this was my first relationship, it was probably typical relationship behavior, ignoring the fact that none of my friends with partners had FaceTime calls glued to their hands 24/7. In my friend group I was surrounded by happy friends in what at least appeared to be strong relationships. I was the most successful professionally, but emotionally I was an outsider because of my abusive relationship. I felt isolated in this reality and didn't talk to my friends about it. My mother had relationships with men, and I observed them my entire life. But they were never hostile or controlling or angry. I told myself Mom was different.

As an outsider there were many seasons in my life where I was brutally aware that I didn't have what others did: health insurance, a home, family vacations, two parents in the home. The list was long. The association between "being an outsider" and "going without" gelled and poisoned my view of what I deserved in a relationship. Ken and I weren't super happy, we argued all the time, but maybe that's all I could get. Maybe that's all I deserved, I thought.

Not having a father figure around and watching men come in and out of my mother's life inconsistently made me an outsider next to all those friends who had two stable parents bringing them up together. I believed being an outsider in that way was a bad thing.

But I was beginning to realize that this wasn't necessarily a deficiency. It was something I could use to make sure I only let the very best, worthy men into my life. This point of difference could be used to my advantage. I would be more aware and intentional about the men I brought into my life.

But this rational take on a very emotionally heightened situation wasn't apparent to me right away. A person can convince themselves to believe whatever they really *want* to believe. And with Ken, it was more comfortable to believe my relationship was perfectly healthy and balance the emotions of frustration and sadness that came with dealing with someone so controlling than to risk an unknown bag of emotions that came with breaking up with him. How does that old saying go? I preferred the devil I knew. The unknown was scary. I couldn't prepare for the unknown. Ironically, my warped perspective on staying with Ken made me think I was *more* in control of my emotional state and less affected by my childhood wounds.

More and more memories of Ken's ambivalent attitude toward my personal goals flooded my mind as I sipped on martini number two. When I celebrated one year of moving off Stacy's couch and getting my own apartment, he didn't join in the festivities. Instead, he was irritated. I wanted to spend a whole evening with my girlfriends doing something that didn't involve him. I felt guilty when I threw that party. Guilty! For a milestone I'd accomplished. When Babes hit six figures in sales for the first time, Ken didn't bat an eye. He didn't even fix his mouth to say congratulations. I deserved better than that. Heat rose on the back of my neck, my cheeks flushed, embarrassed just remembering how stupid I'd been. Dinner that night could have gone entirely differently without Ken's deadweight. Not only was he not loving me in a way that was healthy and affirming, I realized the warped toxic love he held over me like a guillotine was not helping me build myself *or* my business. But knowing I deserved better wasn't enough. I had to *act* as if I knew it.

I pressed back in my chair, digging my heels into the carpet.

Deadweight doesn't propel you forward.

It holds you back.

If Ken wasn't helping me toward my goals, then he was taking me further away from them. There was no neutral. Ken was baggage. Because the absence of my father was baggage. I had a lot of unpacking to do. I decided to get out of that relationship.

And I did, in a month's time.

But *not* the way I expected.

I was at a photoshoot for a new line of dresses I was about to launch. After two hours of setting up the shoot, getting the girls' hair and makeup done and my photographer starting with a series of test shots, the doors to the warehouse burst open.

"We need to talk," Ken said, shoving past me without greeting anyone. His tone was deadened in that way it got when he was really pissed. He wasn't a yeller. But his presence in that warehouse felt like passing close to the eye of a hurricane. I was accustomed to tap dancing around eggshells in response to his mood, so nerves twisted in my stomach. I wasn't sure what he was upset about. I hadn't yet worked up the courage to confront him about how unhappy I was. And though I'd been thinking about ending the relationship, I still wasn't aware of how toxic it was and how I was feeding into those unhealthy habits. But suffice it to say, when Ken barged into my shoot demanding we talk, I immediately felt as if *I'd* done something wrong. I was terrified.

He accused me of cheating—big surprise (I hadn't). Things unraveled from there. He broke up with me that same day after the longest fight of my life. (Verbal, not physical.) At first, breaking myself free from him felt like bobbing along without an anchor at sea. I felt lost, abandoned, my emotions and my brain were completely out of sync. The first day without my toxic boyfriend, I lay in bed all day and did nothing. The second day I talked to his mom. She was always so nice. By the fourth day, I still hadn't eaten. The entire time, my body *knew* this was a good thing, but my heart was lying. I was sad and missed him while simultaneously relieved I didn't have to endure his treatment anymore. Part of me was bothered because the breakup was unjust. I do not like being accused of things I didn't do. It felt unfair. How was *I* the problem in this relationship? But I realized Ken was never going to see things my way. Even his rejection had control over me. By day five I took a steamy shower and stepped out of there, dressed up, got my makeup professionally done, and told myself I'd given him enough of my energy.

I realize now that I should have actively cut Ken out of my life much sooner. That I am deserving of *much* more than he offered. I hadn't realized how he was zapping my energy dry. Energy that could have been used on my professional and personal goals, on myself, or on other people who were deserving of my time and energy.

But if growing up on the outside—the kid *without,* who didn't have the life experiences others did—taught me anything, it was how to pivot and move on. Disappointment, setbacks, heartache, and insert whatever your negative experience of choice is, all of it was something I was well acquainted with. Whether you were marginalized because of poverty like me, or for your gender, religious affiliation, your upbringing, your race, or something else—you, too, know what it's like to deal with and get over negative experiences associated with just existing. This can sometimes lead to us *expecting* to be disappointed. I often struggled with this and still do occasionally, because it's easier to expect to be disappointed than believe you'll succeed. Nevertheless, the gem buried in this unfortunate habit pattern is that bouncing back from adversity can become a well-mastered skill.

Have you ever seen a kid with everything they could possibly want being told no for the first time? Or how about when that kid grows up and runs his first Fortune 500 company only to realize he is beholden to his stockholders and *can't* actually do whatever he wants? Imagine it. It's not a pretty picture, is it? (I'm actually cringing. Are you cringing?) Dusting yourself off and getting back up again is *not* something that comes easy to everyone, especially those who aren't accustomed to being marginalized. At a very early age I grew accustomed to scaling the mountains of disappointment life threw at me. We had to get up the next day and believe it could be easier, better, full of more opportunities. That's how we persisted those years.

After Ken, I'd learned my lesson. It was time to bounce back. I pulled up my sorely neglected work email and started going through it. Then I whipped out a paper calendar that I'd bought months earlier with plans to map out my marketing campaigns well in advance. Planning social media posts is so helpful. But babysitting Ken's insecurities took up so much time and energy that the wall calendar still had the plastic wrap on it. I ripped it off and got to work.

The clock read 3:00 a.m. by the time I finished. I stood and surveyed my handiwork. I'd packed up thirty influencer mailings in cute packaging with Babes goodies, combed through probably a thousand emails, and updated my website. My stomach reminded me I should probably eat something. I wasn't tired; I was exhilarated. I felt so productive, crossing off so many things I'd been needing to do for months.

The next morning was day one of my new marketing campaign. I headed to a poppin' spot for brunch and to take my planned shots of new outfits for social media. By early afternoon, I shared them online. (The night before, I'd spent a few hours doing more research on Instagram hashtags and how the algorithm had changed recently. I really deep dive and nerd out on things when I have the time. And suddenly I had all the time in the world.) God, it felt good to be free! I was done being stagnant. I was moving forward. My steps felt lighter or something. I felt different.

As I packed up from my brunch spot, my phone notifications started going berserk. I swiped up and my jaw hit the floor. I had a series of messages from friends claiming that Kim Kardashian was photographed leaving James Harden's all-white party wearing a Babes dress. My hand shook as I tapped the links to see for myself. I fell back into the seat I'd just emptied at that restaurant. I immediately opened my laptop and fell down the rabbit hole of amplifying this *huge* moment for my business. This kind of press could be a game changer. I'd been going since 7:00 a.m. It was almost 4:00 p.m. If I was with Ken, he'd have been pitching a fit about me being gone so long, making me tell him what I was doing every few minutes. But free Ciera had her whole day to herself. I deserved this!

If any of this journey of mine feels familiar to you, pause and sit with that discomfort. Face it. The successful person you are becoming is on the other side of this mountain. Recognize if the people in your life are propelling you forward or pulling you backward. Choose to give your time, energy, and emotions to those who build you up and push you to be who you intend to be. Toxic people are deadweight. Cut them loose and soar.

THE OUTSIDE SCOOP

I Trusted My Gut When Something Felt Bad

After my breakup, I constantly wrestled with how I could endure something so incredibly awful for so long. I never arrived at an answer, but I wanted to ensure that I would never again find myself in a relationship or situation like that, where I am being manipulated and taken advantage of right under my nose. That thing people say about hindsight being 20/20 really is true. I made a list of the red flags that I ignored. It's interesting that those bright-red flags were very camouflaged at the time. I cycled through each moment where I should have had a wake-up call and tried to remember what excuse I'd told myself. And in almost every instance, I realized that deep down, in my gut, I knew his behavior wasn't okay. I muffled that inner voice often. But I vowed then to always trust my gut in the future. If something doesn't feel right or feels off, trust that intuition and do the brave thing—confront it. As you examine the people and entities (yes, that includes toxic workplace environments, volunteer organizations, social groups) you are giving energy to while on this success journey, can you see any red flags? If so, dig into them.

If there's a relationship (a friendship, business partnership, or romantic one) holding you back for whatever reason, think deeply about whether you need it in your life. Chances are, as soon as you intentionally close the door on a bad relationship and accept what you deserve, another door will open and a better, more fulfilling and fruitful relationship will be waiting on the other side.

I Harnessed the Power of Belief

I needed to believe in my aspirations for my business; just like at the Spike Lee party I needed to believe that I could turn heads when I walked into a room because of how unique my style was. I am in the fashion business; people admiring my clothes is the gateway to building my business. I realized after the breakup with Ken just how powerful belief is. As I reflected on the time working for my mother's store, I could see that people wrapped themselves in their beliefs and they became like an armor, just as I'd wrapped myself in the experiences of my toxic relationship, telling myself it was probably fine.

After Ken I decided, since I am capable of believing anything, that I would choose to believe I am worthy of relationships that would build me up, not ones that tear me down. Whether this feels true or not in the moment, it is a truth I would hold fast to. It would be my armor. Whether with family, friends, or partners, a relationship involves an emotional investment. I would weigh the cost against that standard from then on out to make sure each relationship was worthy of me. Because I am worth a lot. And I deserve self-love, acceptance, a healthy relationship, respect. Not because of what I accomplished, but just because I exist. My worth comes with my humanity. Once I realized that, it was like a tether to my past had been broken.

What parts of your past are keeping you in bondage? What beliefs about yourself and your life do you need to rewrite to truly free yourself? In what areas of your life, personal or professional, are you accepting less than you deserve?

5

—

Realize You're Not the Only Outsider

AFFIRMATION

I am not alone

Kim Kardashian was wearing Babes.

Her picture popped up on a blog, photographed by paparazzi in my white turtleneck sleeveless maxi, leaving a James Harden all-white party. I blinked, but the picture didn't change. I reached out to a friend who ran in circles with Kim's stylist. Once I'd acquired the stylist's email, I reached out to confirm that the dress was indeed Babes. I also thanked them and asked for an address where I could send more dresses. They confirmed that it was my dress and she'd purchased it herself on my site! A few days after that conversation, Kim shared a picture on her own social media page of her in the same dress in the mocha shade (one of the gifts that I sent). She wore it with a champagne satin blazer. A week or so after that, Kim shared another picture of her in my Babes all-black bodysuit styled with a shawl-type cover over it. I was still in pure shock. How was this real?

At this time in 2013, Kim's name dominated headlines. She was pregnant with her first child and the media was full of criticism over how "fat" she was getting. Headlines such as KIM KARDASHIAN "CRIED ALL THE WAY HOME" OVER MET GALA DRESS and KIM KARDASHIAN GAVE WORLD "MIDDLE FINGER" WITH BABY-WEIGHT LOSS were everywhere. One article quoted her saying, "I was gaining weight because I was pregnant, and it was just really hard to read all these stories and hear all these nasty things." Kim's body was changing because she was growing a new life *inside* it. But she'd previously been heralded as a beauty icon because of her curvy, slender frame, so when she no longer fit that mold, she was socially accosted and criticized. She was pushed to the margins in the minds of those who'd worshipped her beauty because she no longer fit their definition. At that moment, Kim was on the outside, like so many women. And Babes, a brand all about celebrating women's bodies, met her there. It is still incredible to me that anyone would ridicule a woman's beauty because of her size—ever. But especially a pregnant woman. It was giving straight-stick-figure obsession. And it took me back to the spring of my senior year of high school when I was shopping for a prom dress.

It was the early 2000s. The post–Spice Girls obsession era. And my mom and my aunt were taking me prom dress shopping. But not at a thrift store. At an actual department store. The inside was *fancy*. I remember thinking the clothes were astronomically priced. But I gulped down my nerves and told myself that this one day, I deserved to feel more beautiful and special than ever before. It was *prom*!

Mom started with her fashionista montage. She pulled a dozen dresses off the racks for me to try on. I grabbed my own. The dressing room clerk was so excited for me, that she let us take in double the amount of clothes.

"Come out when you get the first one on, okay?" Mom shouted from outside the dressing room for the fifth time.

I slipped my favorite one off the hanger first. It was a blue sparkly dress with a mermaid cut. I unzipped it and stepped inside and began to pull it up. It stopped at my thighs. I bit my lip, tugging. But it hardly budged. I sighed and held it over the door.

"Too small. Can you get a bigger size?"

Mom hurried off dutifully as I slipped into another one. This one was black and backless. It had a bit more stretch, and it was an extra large—despite my being five foot two. It made it over my thighs, and I slipped the shoulder straps on. And my boobs popped right out of the top. The fabric that hugged me so well on my pear-shaped bottom half was way too much for my A-cup top half.

"Here," Mom said, and blue fabric flew over the door. "That's the biggest size they have."

I didn't even give the black dress another thought. It's like the designer of that dress didn't realize bodies come in various shapes. I was accustomed to thrifting where I could mix and match pieces and amend them to fit how I wanted. I hadn't ever considered there could be a downside of walking into a store and grabbing something off the rack. The larger size of the blue dress was really long. Like so long it kept tangling between my legs. But I was able to get it over my butt. It was supposed to have a fitted bust, but instead it looked like someone wanted to give me enough room to stuff a ten-piece chicken meal in my shirt.

"Are you coming out?"

"No." I took off the dress and tried on five or six others before I'd had it. They did not fit. My shape wasn't "normal" enough to be designed for, I guess. These dresses must be working for someone. But that someone wasn't me. My clothing needs pushed me to the margins. I once again found myself on the outside of mainstream.

"Mammas, everything all right?"

"Mommy, let's just go." I was disappointed. This was supposed to be a special moment and it just wasn't. I handed the clerk the dresses.

"Did any of these work out?"

"Nope, not one," I told her and we left.

In the end, we managed to thrift a gold dress, which we made some adjustments to. I had a great time at prom and my dress didn't end up mattering as much as I'd hoped it would. But what stuck with me was how that huge store was *full* of clothes but only for one sort of shape. And that shape wasn't mine. My friends in high school had curvy bodies like I did. Their dress searches weren't a shoo-in fit either. Our body shapes rendered us on the outside of mainstream fashion. My problem fitting the mold wasn't just mine. Others were in the same predicament. I was not alone.

—

It was comforting then and again now, as I stared at my phone blowing up with people messaging me about Kim in my clothes, that I was not alone in my awful prom shopping experience. That in these margins, with my big butt and thin waist, with my shelter-insecure background, with my unhealthy relationship patterns, with every marginalizing experience—being on the outside did not and does not mean it's just me. Kim *freaking* Kardashian, with infinite resources, also could not walk into a store, whether Dillard's, Neiman Marcus, or Versace, and find something off the rack that fit as if it were made for her, pregnant or not. Most clothes, then, were not designed for curvy bodies. If a billionaire entrepreneur and socialite with anything she wants at her fingertips could be an outsider, anyone can. I tapped my phone and zoomed in on my dress, noticing the way it hugged Kim's gorgeous belly and cinched in all the right places. She was beautiful, headlines be damned.

At the time, my designs for Babes were created from my own personal needs. The first pair of pants I'd thrifted had a gap in the back. I have a very rotund behind. So when I hand sewed those pants to fit better, I specifically tailored them so the back fabric wouldn't gape above my butt. I wanted the fabric to lay down across my swayed back instead of revealing my underwear. As my business grew to cater to cut-and-sew pieces and moved away from vintage thrifting, my tendency was to design clothes that worked for a large back end, a thin waist, and a modest bust. I was designing for me. And I knew there were other women who looked like me. They were my customers—pear-shaped, big-booty girls, with small waists and chests. I stared at Kim K's maternity photo. She and I have more things that set us apart than we have in common. We aren't the same ethnicity, race, or socioeconomic class. But as my body developed and dipped and curved, my needs, as a woman, were the same as hers. If my brand could meet Kim's needs, a person with the world at her fingertips, that meant it could meet *many* more women's needs than I'd first imagined.

As crazy as it sounds, this situation helped me realize that I am not isolated in my way of seeing the world. There are others who operate from the margins as I do. Passively I understood this, but I didn't see the power in recognizing it until that moment. *Big things happen when outsiders find common ground and connect.* There is power in shared experiences, and how you can benefit from it will depend on what sort of success you're chasing. Perhaps just knowing there are other mothers with PTSD in your social network is empowering. Or knowing there are fellow women at your workplace who have been hungry for a promotion but have found themselves constantly passed over. The awareness that each other exists affirms that you are not isolated; it creates opportunities for collaboration and sharing resources. As a business owner, I had focused on people who were outsiders exactly like me, but there were more outsiders out there I could be designing for! For the entrepreneurial-minded who are starting a business to address a problem, learn from my mistake: find your broader outsider audience, not just the people who are very similar to you. (Your audience may not even be you at all. The person who owns Fashion Nova is a dude.)

Kim showed me how varied outsiders are and how Babes could be transformed by that fact. After that, I began designing clothes for various sizes—women with pregnant bellies, apple-shaped bodies, narrower hips than mine. I also added models in various races, ethnicities, and body types to my collection launches. My brand has evolved to encompass my customers' growing needs. Many found me before they had children, then came back when they were pregnant and invested in my lines that work well for maternity. Postpartum through working out to lose the baby weight, they come back time and time again because Babes has shown that it is a brand that will grow with them. That sort of forward-thinking vision strengthened Babes's roots and helped me get closer to the company I was trying to build in the first place.

Open your eyes to the fact that you are not alone in the ways you do not fit in. There are lots of outsiders out there and in places you wouldn't necessarily expect. Connect with them and watch the success in your life grow as you're supported and empowered with a widened field of view. And recognize that the moves you make to better yourself are moves that are also going to help other people. Whether you're fighting for inclusivity and representation at work or convincing your boss to change the company's marketing strategy to an approach you have a strong vision for, you may feel like you're on an island of ideas by yourself, but you're not. You are not alone and there is power in seeing and using that to transform how you hustle toward your goals.

THE OUTSIDE SCOOP

I Told Someone about My Wildest Ambitions

Long ago, in the early dregs of Babes, when I was sewing together pieces of clothes on a sofa at Stacy's house, I'd subconsciously set a goal for myself to succeed as an entrepreneur and break the cycle of generations of poverty and home insecurity in my family lineage. Years later I was doing okay, but I hadn't reached the pinnacle of the success I believed I could attain. I didn't own a home, for example. So I decided right then to tell someone that I was going to own a home someday and build sustainable wealth to leave to my children to further their lineages. I think my friend burst out laughing because I'm not usually super open with my feelings. This book is more honest than I've ever been with myself out loud. So she was shocked at my honesty. But there was something, call it iron-willed resolve perhaps, that made me feel accountable to those words. I *had* to do what I'd said out loud. It was real now. I ended up telling more friends and found a less awkward way to bring it up (read: with humor and dry sarcasm), and the more I did that, not only did I feel more determined but it surprisingly led me to so many like-minded people! Fellow outsiders who were also hungry, driven, and passionate about the same things as me. Sharing my goals aloud made them feel more attainable in more ways than one. I knew I wasn't alone, which made my optimistic ambition feel that much more warranted. My dreams weren't crazy. Others were busting their asses for the same reason!

First, get real with yourself when identifying your goals. What are your goals and where do they come from? What ceilings are you determined to shatter? What patterns in your family history are you determined to break? Or perhaps it's a private, personal battle that's intertwined itself with *why* you're so hungry to succeed? What ultimately drives you to keep turning the pages of this book? What are you *going to* prove to yourself with these personal and professional goals you've set? Now that you know the root of what you're driving toward, say it out loud. And then ask yourself how others can help. Are there other people out there that want the same things as me?

Then, talk to someone (or several someones) about it and connect with people who are or have been where you are. I promise you it will make everything you're working toward seem all the more possible and all the more real. We are not islands. We need other people. You are not alone.

6

It's Okay to Use People

The idea of using people sounds bad at face value. But let me explain.

In 2015, my business was doing quite well. Well enough that I could finally afford my own place. For once in my life, I was excited to have people over. I'd host game nights, wine nights, just-come-over-because-I-want-someone-to-hang-out-with nights. One night, I invited a bunch of people over, close friends and a few newer friends, including Breanna, a girl I'd met on Instagram who was selling an olive bodysuit that she'd cut and designed herself. It was a cute outfit. I think I may have even bought it. But it was her only item. She wasn't exactly a competitor or in business like I was at that point.

As a throng of guests flooded in, I bobbed through the crowd, passing out drinks, making sure everyone was having a good time. Breanna, who'd shown up alone, stuck to my side. Conversation moved from how cute my nails were, to how nice my swanky three-bedroom place in this "very nice" side of town was, and eventually to how business was going. Breanna scooted closer to me on my couch.

"So how do you get the clothes you sell? It's so creative, do you source everything overseas?"

"No, I make everything here."

"Even the simple items? You used to post more one-of-a-kind pieces. How do you make so much at once?"

"Uhhh, it's a lot to explain," I chuckled. "You really want to know?"

She nodded eagerly and waited patiently as I moved around the room to refill my guests' drinks. The truth was my business had evolved considerably in its three years and it had more than quadrupled my income. For starters, I'd moved from thrifting one-of-a-kind outfits to making multiples of the same design. Thrifting outfits became more of an exclusive, separate collection, which I called Babes vintage. The heart of my business became cut and sew and wholesale.

It all started with a random trip to the fashion district to shop when I slipped into a stretchy tube top as a skirt and grabbed a racerback sports bra and put it on backward.

"How many of these do you have?" I asked the shop owner, and she showed me a box of hundreds. "I'll take thirty," I said, the wheels turning. I took some photos of my outfit and shared it on social media, offering the whole outfit for forty-five dollars. All thirty sold out within an hour. The next day I went back and bought out the lady's entire stock of racerbacks and tube tops, realizing I'd just stumbled on a way to sell *way* more product.

I sat back down beside Breanna and decided to explain this whole process to her. By the time I finished, her eyes were wide with awe. She high-fived me and for a moment Breanna seemed as if she were somewhere else. Then she met my eyes and fired off a round of follow-up questions about how many pieces I'd buy at a time and how I negotiated for the best price.

"Girl, are you working me?" I asked with a forced laugh. "You trying to steal my secrets?"

Breanna never answered that question directly. And she didn't need to because three weeks later, a new online fashion retailer popped up on the Los Angeles scene with designs sourced from the exact stores and tailors I used.

Breanna was in business.

For years after that party, I felt naive for sharing so much. And completely betrayed by Breanna. I assumed she wanted to understand my business because she'd dreamed of doing something bigger with hers. But to specifically ask my advice for the purpose of tapping into my resources, negotiating similar terms with my supplier, and copycatting felt icky to me.

The next time I had a party, work talk wasn't allowed. In fact, after that if anyone asked me for tips, I said I didn't have any—ha! I shut myself off from sharing anything and I grew more hesitant to invite anyone into my circle of trust. I only let people get close to me once I knew them very well. No one would put one over on me like Breanna did, I used to tell myself.

Eventually Breanna's following on social media grew and she began to develop her own brand, which was admittedly very different from mine. She catered more to the trendy market and had sexier "hype" pieces. She also designed for more narrow-framed girls, whereas Babes catered to highlighting women's natural curves. I noticed the subtle differences between our brands, but it didn't matter. Swiping past her page got an irritated eye roll from me every single time.

Until three years later.

It was 2018.

My basics collections were still doing really well. But it felt like I'd reached a sort of earning plateau. So I was working on brainstorming bigger and better ways to increase my brand visibility. I had clever ideas, such as sending celebrities samples of my clothes, hoping they would like them enough to wear them in public or post about them on social media like Kim had done organically. But celebrities have no shortage of free things thrust at them, so sending off these mailings once a month felt like shouting in a crowded room. I would spend hours researching publicists, packing products beautifully, and including handwritten notes, hoping that this would break through the clutter.

I had been very close friends with a guy, we'll call him Niles, since I'd moved to Los Angeles in 2012. And we finally decided to try a romantic relationship. He is a songwriter and well connected. He's written for Bruno Mars and Rihanna, to name a few. He's also just really nice. Being so well connected, he was a wealth of suggestions and ideas. (He wasn't like Ken at all. He and I had a friendship that undergirded our relationship, and he always regarded me with respect.) When my business succeeded, he was the first person to hype and to celebrate with me. In fact, when my business exploded after Kim Kardashian posted my outfit for the first time, Niles was one of the first to reach out to congratulate me. Despite his support, I was always hesitant to ask for connections to his clients or friends. I didn't want to be his Breanna.

Like one time we were at dinner and his phone started buzzing nonstop.

"Oh, shit. I have to go. Can you drop me off somewhere?"

We'd driven in my car that night.

"Of course, what's wrong?"

"Rihanna wants to meet up about this song we're working on. *Now.*"

My fork wrapped in buttery fettuccini halted at my mouth. *Damn, I wish I could get my clothes to her,* I thought. But I didn't say anything about wishing I could meet Rihanna at that moment. We grabbed our food to go, and I dropped him off at the studio. When Niles returned to his place later that night, we were talking about how it went at the studio and again I considered asking if he could give Rihanna some of my clothes the next time they linked up. Or mention me to her or something.

"I was thinking—"

"Yeah?" He thrummed his guitar, and I tucked in the covers, chewing my lip so hard it actually hurt. Breanna came to mind immediately. My stomach soured as I remembered how used I felt when she exploited her access to me to help her business goals.

"Never mind," I said. I wasn't an opportunist. I would never want Niles to feel like Breanna made me feel.

Niles's and my relationship grew from there. I really thought I was going to marry this guy at one point. But a little over a year and a half later, we broke up. And it had nothing to do with me trying to access his connections. That never happened. It was just one of those couple mix-ups that went sideways. We're still friends to this day. He's reached out several times to tell me how dope my business appears to be doing. Or just to see how I'm doing. And when my mom got sick, he reached out to make sure I was good. Niles wanted the best for me, whether we were together or not.

It was then that I realized, had I asked Niles to introduce me to his robust celebrity network, he would have done it without hesitation because he knew I wasn't in the relationship to use him. Seeing how he genuinely wanted me to succeed, whether we were dating or not, made me realize he knew how genuine my feelings were for him, too.

I thought of Breanna again and how her brand was flourishing, completely unrelated to Babes. Truthfully, she wasn't really competition for my business because her customers weren't necessarily mine. It had been three years since that wine night in my apartment and I could honestly say she really wasn't taking money out of my pocket. Though for years I'd been too stubborn to see it that way. Breanna had carved out her own niche but used me as a stepping stone to get the doors open. And in that moment, after Niles and I had broken up and I considered all the opportunities he would have happily exposed me to, I could finally, definitively admit that what Breanna did wasn't necessarily a bad thing.

I should have used Niles's connections to get ahead. I should have packaged up a box and asked him to give it to Rihanna the next time they were in the studio. I should have asked him to introduce me to some of his business partners. In terms of connections in LA, Niles was squarely on the inside. I was the outside. How much further ahead would my business have been if I did? I'll never know. But I learned my lesson and decided the next time I could ethically take advantage of someone, I would do it much differently by being straightforward and honest about my intentions.

The opportunity came a few months later at a baby shower at a beautiful scenic overlook in West Hollywood. My ears perked up when I overheard someone talking about some design work they'd done. Graphic design was an area of weakness for me. I'd taught myself how to use a digital camera, edit photos, and work with lighting, but putting together aesthetically pleasing promotional graphics was where I hit a dead end. I could have hired someone, of course. But I'm cheap, *duh*, so I didn't. I'd much prefer to learn how to do it myself so that way it isn't a constant expense. I inserted myself in their conversation, pretending I was just wandering over.

"I'm Ciera." I shook both women's hands, but I had my eyes on the shorter, curly haired one I'd heard talking.

"Nice to meet you. I'm Bianca."

"What's your IG?" In my experience networking, getting someone's social media handle was the easiest way to figure out who they were.

I tapped her handle into the app and brought up her profile. My heart twinged. "Jewelry and Graphic Design Artist." At that moment, I decided I wanted to be her friend. Because I wanted to learn everything she knew about graphic design.

"Oh, you're a fashion designer," she said, tapping on her phone, apparently eyeing my profile. "Nice."

I needed to get her alone.

"So, how do you know the guest of honor?" I asked, and before I knew it Bianca and I were having an entire conversation and the third wheel in our conversation wandered off to refresh her drink. "We should get together sometime." I did want to hang out with her, not to become besties but because she had a cool job and I was curious about learning from her about her business. I wanted to tap into her skills and resources. I hoped she would share them with me. In the world of graphic design, I was a nobody, completely on the outside with nothing to contribute. Bianca had the know-how, the skills. Graphic design was her world and I wanted to dip my toe in it. I didn't have anything to offer her as a clothing designer. So swapping services, like I did back in my early styling days, didn't seem appropriate. I thought of Breanna. And Niles. I would be straight up with her. I bit my lip and shuffled my feet. We talked and walked a little longer before I dropped the bomb on her, "I want to hear more about what you do."

Her brow rose. "Oh?"

"I want you to teach me everything you know about graphic design."

She laughed. I didn't. "You're serious."

"Yep."

Her smile grew. "Well, all right, sure. Why not?"

About a month later Bianca and I finally had time in our schedules that aligned. I showed up at her house and what proceeded was a whole day of her showing me the ins and outs of graphic design. The rule of thirds, how to use InDesign. It was a lot of information, but I ate it all up. I honestly felt like I should probably be paying her. But I was and am all about free resources. When the session wrapped up, I turned to her, and said, "Thanks for all this. I saw that you were a designer at that baby shower, and I was like, I need to get to know her now and learn how she does what she does."

Honest.

Transparent.

"Girl," she said with a chuckle between her words. "When I saw how big your following was, I wanted to get as close to you as possible to boost my jewelry line."

I burst out laughing and we toasted our matchas. From that moment forward Bianca and I became great friends.

If I could go back in time to when I was with Niles, I would have been up front about my insecurity of how he'd view me. I would have told him about what Breanna did to me. Because what I know now is that the way you go about using someone matters more than the fact that you used them. I was a complete opportunist when I met Bianca. And so was she! We wanted to tap into each other's wisdom and resources. But I was up front about my intentions, which shielded our relationship from misunderstanding and miscommunication and allowed it to blossom even more beneficially. With Bianca I practiced what I like to call ethical opportunism.

An opportunist is someone who exploits circumstances for their benefit. An ethical opportunist is someone who exploits circumstances transparently, with integrity and compassionate intent. As an outsider, I know what it feels like to be a crab in a barrel, trampled over as others claw their way up and over me. I'd never want to cause anyone to feel that way. The goal of the ethical opportunist is not to ignore opportunities but to grab hold of them without burning bridges, damaging relationships, or causing undue harm to the person being taken advantage of. The purpose isn't to hurt their position, but to better yours. And as long as I do just that, there is no reason to hesitate.

If you can get resources from a person without being intentionally deceitful, malicious, or inflicting harm, why should that person feel taken advantage of? Remember, you are building on everything you can get your hands on. That includes the things you have access to in your network. Whether that person holds on to a grudge for three years as I did or applauds you for being strategic, their reaction isn't within your control. Who knows, they might realize you weren't trying to get in the way of their success at all and recognize you were just trying to carve out your own. Or even that you have skills or knowledge to offer them in return. Breanna missed out on me giving her more. If she were officially my protégé, for example, perhaps we'd have a lifelong business relationship at this point. Perhaps that could have led her to even bigger things. It worked out for her, ultimately, but she also missed an opportunity by not being open and up front with me about her intentions. It doesn't have to be a one-way relationship.

But don't shy away from it when it is. As women, we have been historically conditioned to not step on toes or be imposing. Girl, *be* imposing.

Full stop.

Advocate for yourself. No one else is going to root for you as hard as *you*. I shouldn't have let Breanna's approach stop me from seeking help and using my network's knowledge in the *right* way. She went about her business, just as Niles continued to root for me. My feelings about it were an issue only for me.

From the ambitious moms who want to ensure their kids have a shot at the most exclusive internships or schools to the twenty-somethings without the proper on-paper credentials but all the know-how, do not waste opportunities that come your way. Ethically seize each one. If that requires using people to advance your position in the world, do it.

THE OUTSIDE SCOOP

I Was Not an Asshole

I don't like the feeling I get in my stomach when I upset someone. Some of this is social conditioning, I'm sure. But I used to be very conflict-averse. I still am, for the most part. Except when it comes to being an ethical opportunist. Once I began approaching relationships differently, I did get some side-eye. I also found a lot of people were grateful for the honesty. Others steered clear, as is their right. But there was a small group of people who deemed me rude because of how up front I was. And I started to get that sick feeling in my stomach again. After way too much chocolate, I pulled myself together and reminded myself of why I'm doing what I'm doing. Then I drew a line in the sand, figuratively. I decided that compassion, transparency, and integrity are not the qualities of an asshole. Therefore, I could be confident in the knowledge that I am not an asshole, and if some people did see me that way, it was on them. They would have to work through their feelings as I did with Breanna. I knew who I was and who I wasn't. And I found peace with that.

How do you allow the fear of being judged dictate how hard you hustle for what you want? Are there certain ways you fear being seen? Opportunistic? Aggressive? A know-it-all? Selfish? If you know your intentions are truly pure, own that and block out the rest. It's all noise. Grasping this is critical on the path to success, especially for outsiders.

I Sought Out Opportunities to Use People

With my newfound confidence in how I would approach and engage with people who have something to offer, at first I waited for more opportunities to come to me. I'm not sure what I expected—someone to walk up to me and go on and on about their million-dollar philanthropic efforts and how they were itching to shower someone (me) with them. But this never happened. This doesn't happen. Once I realized I couldn't just idly wait around for people to come to me, I began to *look* for opportunities to use people. (I know how that sounds, but you know that I mean ethically so I'm not going to beat that drum again.) I began introducing myself openly to people and making it clear that I'm always looking for opportunities to grow and network. When someone introduces themselves to me, I'll ask probing questions about what they do. I allow the wheels to turn in my mind and I'll really spend time thinking about how I could benefit from their wealth of knowledge. Sometimes, I can't. And that's fine. For the record—my group of friends and my personal network are not groups of people I leech off. I am not a bloodsucking parasite, and this isn't a sci-fi novel. I am, however, an ambitious go-getter who knows who she is and what she wants. And I won't apologize for that or act like I'm someone else.

And when the chance arises for me to share my knowledge with someone who wants to honestly and transparently use me, I'm happy to help.

7

Focus On Your Own Version of Success

AFFIRMATION

If I am making progress toward my goals, I am successful

I'm a coffee-before-I-can-people person.

Once I'm caffeinated, I bounce around like the Energizer Bunny. But on photoshoot days, the adrenaline pumping through my body is its own double shot of espresso. So when I woke up the morning of a modeling photoshoot fit for the gods in summer 2019, I could hardly sit still, bursting at the seams with excitement. This shoot was going to change everything! It was so over the top. I'm talking floor-to-ceiling paned glass windows in a modern industrial warehouse with sweeping tall ceilings, exposed brick, and glossed cement floors. There was flawless light and I brought props such as vases, which I never did. But the biggest change was that for the very first time I'd be working with *real* models from the top-notch talent agency LA Models.

By then, I had been bringing in a steady six figures a month. It started as a slow build as I shifted from reworking existing pieces to creating my own designs and hiring tailors to bring them to life. Eventually I moved away from thrifting almost completely. I still remember what I was wearing the day I saved my first $5,000. My account was negative most of my life before then. And when it wasn't I was working paycheck to paycheck. So that milestone felt *huge*. People don't talk about the seemingly small goals. But those small goals are not small at all. Every step makes the next one seem more possible. I'd saved $5K, which meant I was capable of saving $10K, $100K, and so on.

I attribute a lot of my swift growth to my Instagram growth. Within a few months I went from starting an IG account to having 20,000 followers. (Which was *a lot* back then.) There just wasn't anyone doing what I was doing on Instagram at that time. In a filter-obsessed era, I was selling clothes using myself as a model *without* filters, *without* editing out my cellulite or back rolls. My brand resonated. That scarcity brought lots of customers my way.

But I was eager to grow even more. I perused other designers' websites, such as Nasty Gal, Wolford, and a few others. The difference between our website shopping experiences was minimal. We all had clean designs and easy-to-navigate shopping sections, which could be categorized by item. We all used social media, though I leaned more heavily on it. The main difference I noticed was that other successful fashion brands used professional models, which gave their websites a certain aesthetic. I couldn't quite put my finger on what I'd call the vibe, but there was a distinct *look* other fashion brands' websites had. And then there was mine: crowded, full of competing colors, and inconsistent photo editing. It looked like a struggle DIY project. Gone were the early years in my business when Spike Lee was just urging me to have a website at all. Now that I'd made it to my competitors' playing field financially, I needed it to *look* the part.

The morning of the shoot, makeup artists, hairstylists, and photographers buzzed around, gearing up for a full day of shooting. Photoshoots were exciting. It felt like creating art. And *this* art was going to make a statement unlike any I'd made before. *This* art would show that I'd fully arrived because it would put me on par, visually, with other top brands in my industry.

The day went flawlessly. No outfit snafus, no technical issues. The edited images arrived from the photographer later that night. I hurried to my office to look at them.

I opened the first file and cocked my head, taking it all in. The silk knee-length skirt draped over the model's angular, sharp body like fine fabric slung over an ornately carved statue. The photograph of this line didn't look like anything like I'd ever produced before. The girls I typically used for shoots were everyday women, full of dips and curves. Much like my own body. I often modeled my clothes myself or shared customer images because that was vastly cheaper and more efficient than hiring anyone. But no one was logging onto Wolford's website and seeing pictures of the owner modeling clothes. Or a smattering of unscripted customer pictures.

This new aesthetic looked like a professional advertising campaign instead of an everyday girl walking the streets of LA. Partially because most modeling agencies featured traditional model shape—five eleven and very thin.

"These girls look incredible," I reassured myself as I began loading the images into my website instead of waiting until the next day. Partly because I'd spent so much money hiring those models and was anxious to see some profit. But also because I was just excited. It took a few hours and coordination of all sorts of mind-numbing things like checking hyperlinks, syncing each item with its appropriate picture, and some minor website adjustments to spotlight the new line on my landing page. But eventually with cramped fingers from gripping my mouse for so many hours, I clicked PUBLISH SITE.

As the page refreshed, I leaned into my screen, eyeing my handiwork. Then I shared the new line on my social media and tapped refresh. It usually took less than a minute for a hundred or so Likes. A few minutes passed and the post had a handful of Likes. Like literally three. Something was obviously wrong with my phone. I set it aside and scrolled through my website. The images of the new skirt and top stuck out among the other clothes on the site. I shifted in my seat realizing *how* much it stuck out . . . like a mismatched pair of shoes. My heart thumped. I checked my social media again. Five minutes had passed. Six Likes. *Six*.

My stare at the pink silk top turned to glare. Something was wrong. My site, the top of it at least where the new line of dresses was featured, looked just like the bigger-name designers' websites did. Aesthetically, I was there. Why weren't people responding to me the way they did to them?! Where were my sales? An hour passed and normally I'd see a rush of orders, twenty to thirty within the first thirty minutes of a new launch. But a full hour later, there were still zero. None. *It's not working. My customers aren't buying.* Another hour passed and only a trickle of sales came in. My line launches typically sold out within a day. The trajectory of this line's performance was headed for the toilet. After hours in my office, I couldn't do anything but pace, replaying everything I'd done over and over in my head. Until I was nudged with an eerily familiar feeling. *I've been here before.*

My later middle school years were some of my most impressionable. I remember them so vividly, the highs and the lows, because many of them were formative, and some were downright scarring. At fourteen, I was finally comfortable at Gregory-Lincoln middle because I'd attended for two consecutive school years. Rare for me, a kid who moved around a lot. My cheerleader friends were popular. So I was adjacently popular, too, even though I couldn't dress exactly like them. I fit in with them in every other way as best as I could. But when Mom had saved up some extra money to take us shoe shopping at a budget retail shoe store called Payless instead of Goodwill, I wasn't going to miss the chance to sport the trending style at the time: K-Swiss. If you're thinking, *I didn't know Payless sold brand name shoes*, hold on to your pants.

"You're absolutely sure these are the ones you want?" My mom pressed her hand to her hip eyeing the box of crisp white K-Swiss tennis shoes I'd taken three seconds to find when we entered the store. I saw those familiar white stripes and made a beeline for them. I grabbed a few colored laces, which would be cool to swap out to match my clothes on non-uniform days. They were genuinely cute shoes. And also happened to be the shoes *everyone* was wearing. They were the hotness. I could finally stop pretending to belong in my friend group and actually belong. Because if outwardly I looked like they did, that's what that meant. I would be one of them. To fourteen-year-old me, this was soundproof logic.

We checked out and the next day I couldn't get to school fast enough. I stepped out of Mom's car and strutted into school like

Alicia Silverstone in *Clueless*. You couldn't tell me anything. I was in my red and khaki uniform and my hair was styled in a rolled-sock bun. The hallway bustled with students as usual, and more were looking my way. Up first at my hair then down to my shoes. I didn't give the stares much attention, skimming the crowd for my friends. But it was the football players who spotted me first.

"Sup, shorty. Rockin' the—"

I curled my lips in a smirk, ready for the designer's names on his lips.

"*Fake*-Swiss. Aye yo, Mac, look. Ciera got them four stripes." He guffawed.

Time seemed to still. Suddenly all the eyes in the hallway burned my skin. My feet wouldn't move.

"What are you talking about, Reggie?"

He turned his own shoe to the side. His friend, the quarterback for the eighth-grade team, joined us and angled his shoe sideways. Five stripes. K-Swiss had *five* stripes. Not four! I went cold all over, trying to swallow and find words. But only an "Uhhh . . ." came out. I rushed past them when I knocked into my friend.

"You okay?" Her eyes fell to my feet before I'd said anything. She bit her lip in sympathy, her brows cinched. Apparently, the news spread fast. Gregory-Lincoln had turned into my funeral. I put those shoes in my closet and never looked at them again. The epitome of success in school is popularity, not grades, in case you didn't know. And I'd tried emulating the *look* of "success" on display by others. I failed miserably.

Now here I was again, two decades later, dealing with the same problem. Trying to put on the aesthetic, as I understood it, of success. The reality is that I liked those shoes. They were the nicest shoes I owned. They were comfortable, too. And because we did a lot of walking most days, going to work with my mom after we got out of school, comfort was king. They were also representative of so much more than shoes. My mom was able to take me shopping at a store and let me pick out whatever I wanted. That was huge. That was progress. That suggested that things in my life could be moving in a more stable, successful direction. But none of that mattered. The shoes didn't look like the success I was aiming for.

I scrolled through my website with this memory weighing heavily on my mind and opened some of my older product images. Several of these were poorly lit. The models I used didn't wear high-fashion makeup, nor was the background stylized at all. But it offered a snapshot of a real person enjoying my clothes in their everyday wardrobe. My jaw ticked as I realized I had been trying to make sure I had the correct number of stripes on my K-Swiss again with this photoshoot.

I wanted to look like the others because I'd bought into the idea that doing what *they* did meant I was truly successful. Instead of finding pride in the outside-the-box way I'd approached marketing, I realized I had been subconsciously discounting all I'd accomplished because of how different my approach was. The truth is my social media images of new collections did best when they included a customer image. People were not buying because of the professional appearance; they were buying because they enjoyed seeing clothes on real, everyday women. That is the brand I'd built in Babes. That is the experience my customers had grown to expect and trust. That method of marketing is how I took myself from being forced to wear free clothes to buying any kind of clothes or shoes I want, whenever I want. My novel approach to marketing represented progress and innovation and success. But at that moment, I couldn't see any of that, and my profits on that very costly line continued to sink.

I let a full two days pass hoping the costs associated with my shoot weren't down the drain. But it was no use. Not only was the line not selling, but I was stalling at thinking of some way to salvage this mess. The silk skirt and top were really cute. That I knew. But my packaging and presentation apparently made my customers feel like it wasn't for them.

It was the middle of the night when I popped up from a deep sleep with an idea. If my outside-the-box ideas to use customers and everyday people as models is what had built Babes, maybe *they* were the answer to fixing this. I reached out to the handful of customers who had bought the outfit and asked them to send in pictures of them wearing it. They did, and I took down my fancy photoshoot photos, revamping the entire appearance of this line on my website using customer images. I published the site and re-shared on socials and my sales picked up almost immediately. By the end of the week, my sales numbers were where I wanted them. Half of my inventory was gone.

With both the K-Swiss and the models, I failed for different reasons. But the issue was the same: copying the popular trend is always a bad idea because no matter how poorly or perfectly you're able to do it, people will spot that you're being inauthentic.

Buying into the idea that success looks a certain way was detrimental to my business and my sense of self. I'd been so caught up in what my business looked like compared to others in the industry, I was missing how incredible my business was *doing in its own right*. Why did my website need to look like other designers' if my business was growing by leaps and bounds? It didn't. But the struggle to define my success by others' standards was deeply ingrained. Because this struggle goes beyond business. It was rooted in my lack of security in being different.

I'd spent my childhood wanting to be like others—to not be the poor kid, the homeless kid, the hungry kid, the kid abandoned by her father. Subconsciously, I hated being in the margins. I wanted to be on the *inside*. I'd nurtured an unintentional habit of chasing others' experiences as *the* standard. I should not have been surprised that this toxic habit of coveting *others'* success clouded my view of my own accomplishments. Thankfully my customers reminded me of *how* we'd built all we'd built together, inspiring me to trust in my own version of success.

Stop worrying about how many stripes are on your K-Swiss. Success doesn't look one way.

When you're building success in an arena where you are an outsider, there's an implicit perception of what it will look like when you arrive. Usually, it's some version of what those *not* on the outside—insiders'—success looks like. These subconscious ideas about how you will know you've hit the official "success" benchmark can be shaped by our own childhood wounds, as they were with me. And until you've reached that arbitrary bar you're striving for, you might not feel successful at all, even when you're accomplishing so much. That's poison to an ambitious spirit because it's downright demotivating.

Knowing that you are making meaningful progress toward your goals can be the difference between persisting when it gets hard and giving up. If you feel like you're spinning your wheels, or the goalpost feels like it continues to move, you risk robbing yourself of motivation. Or, as I've seen with some of my friends, you can become so bitter about the constant exhaustion that you never *sit* in the success you've reached and really breathe it in. I have some friends who are incredible mothers. But I see this *so* often with them. They have all kinds of lofty goals to give their children a childhood full of experiences they never had. But no matter how many milestones their kids blow past, another one pops up in its place. And these tireless, hardworking, badass moms never really sit down and say to themselves, *You're a good fucking mom. You did that.*

As outsiders, we are used to moving within the margins, being the oddball. Our methods, habits, and practices are often different. And if you're like me, you've found comfort in the day-to-day experience of being an outsider. It's your norm. But we need to allow our success to be an outsider, too. It can look different and that's okay because we know better than anyone that different is *good*. If our journey doesn't look like someone else's, then our success may not either. And that does not negate its value and worth. That does not mean we have any less success than the next person. Being an outsider frees us to exist boundlessly, carving our own paths, pioneering. That's something we do better than anyone because we're surrounded by uncharted territory, just like creative ideas shoved to the margins for not being mainstream. When *Twilight* landed on the desks of publishers, the concept of a teenage girl falling in love with a sparkly vampire didn't seem like a typical romance that was going to appeal broadly. It was outside the box, and the world became obsessed. Outside the box is a recipe for success more often than it is not. Curvy girls were historically rejected by mainstream fashion. I made curvy girls' clothes into a million-dollar fashion brand in my own meandering sort of way using social selling, modeling my own clothes, hand stitching, and all sorts of instinctual strategies I'd never seen done by anyone.

We are outsiders.

And we get to define what our success looks like.

THE OUTSIDE SCOOP

I Put Blinders On

It took me a long while to realize that I couldn't compare myself to other brands if I wasn't looking at other brands. I didn't know what Wolford was doing if I wasn't constantly checking their pages. It was a passive obsession where my conscious brain was in cahoots with my subconscious brain to lead me astray. One would lie for the other, telling me that I'm looking at my competitors just to "see what's out there." *Liar!* My subconscious mind was itching to compare what I saw to what I was doing. Once I realized my own brain was working against me, I stopped looking at my competitors. Cold turkey. Just stopped altogether. If I needed to gather research, I'd have someone on my team do it. I kept my eyes on my own paper. I will add that it can be good to look at the competition from time to time to stay aware of what's going on, but that doesn't mean copy what you see.

Break free of comparison culture. To put it another way, when are you most likely to look at what your competition is doing? How does it make you feel? Inspired? Unmotivated? Shitty? If it makes you feel bad, whether it's a friend who is always posting about their milestones, a mom who appears to perpetually have it together, or a business rival who makes you feel sick, consider not following them on social media. Or at least mute them. There are other ways to stay in touch that aren't triggering. Where is your focus as you consider your own success? Where *should* it be? On you. Make intentional choices to keep it there.

I Noticed and Affirmed My Own Success

I have a short memory when it comes to my own success. My brain is hardwired to see problems first, so when I look at the things I've accomplished, my brain automatically minimizes those successes. I'm a big fan of self-affirmation. I knew that if I could own the idea that I am successful it would transform into fuel to keep me going. But to do that I had to unpack my internalized ideas about success and find the root of those preconceived notions. I had to be choosy about which standards of success I dangled from a string. To address this, I began making a list of things I accomplish and committing to talking about these on social media and with friends and family. And I commit to celebrating each one, no matter how seemingly small. There is something about celebrating a success that makes it feel more valid. It also helps remap my brain on how I perceive my accomplishments. I've realized that the more I treat my small wins like a big deal, the more they *feel* like a big deal.

Dig into your success paradigm by asking yourself what misconceptions about success you have swallowed. That's a big question that can be broken down into smaller ones if that's helpful. Start with: What was your earliest idea of success that you can recall? When you say the word "success" aloud, what images come to mind? Is that image what you actually want? If the answer isn't emphatically yes, consider why *that's* the image that comes to mind. Look closely at how external perspectives on success have built the lens through which you view your own success journey. Be honest with yourself: what successes are you minimizing that you should be celebrating?

And finally, draw a line in the sand right now—*go* celebrate them.

8

Teach Yourself to Tackle the Impossible

AFFIRMATION

I can learn to do anything

I answered the FaceTime call and all I could hear was screaming on the other end.

It was December 2018. My mom was outside of a hospital in Houston, on the verge of passing out, so dehydrated and malnourished her lips were cracked, her skin peeling. I was on my couch in Los Angeles gaping at the phone in horror. Her hair was dry, and her clothes didn't match—which might seem like such a small thing to notice, but this was *my* mother, Zoe of Zoe International. The fashionista. Blood was splattered all over her nose and mouth as if she'd eaten a person. It was terrifying. She kept dabbing her nose with a tissue and more blood would pour out. My sister was holding my mother's passenger-side car door open, trying to convince her to get out and go inside. A nurse was standing nearby on the receiving driveway of the hospital with a wheelchair, pleading with her to come in. I couldn't breathe. I couldn't move. Questions raced through my mind. I clumsily tapped my airline app while on the phone, trying to coax my mom to get out of the car. I bought tickets to Houston, my body two steps ahead of my mind at that moment. I could hardly put two words together, but I knew I needed to get from LA to Houston—*and fast.*

Babes was at the height of its success at this point. I was consistently earning seven figures. But the world flipped on its axis that day and this deeply personal moment ended up teaching me one of the most priceless life and business lessons I've ever learned—that I can scale the seemingly insurmountable. That when there is no conceivable way to fix a problem, I will find one.

My hands gripped the seat the entire flight. I didn't say a word to anyone. My brain was still a fog of questions. I stayed on the phone with my mom and sister all the way to the airport. When the plane touched down, I remember clutching my chest as my phone came back on and my sister's missed messages popped up confirming that Mom was still alive and admitted to the hospital.

I rushed to the ICU. When I was in high school, my mother was diagnosed with lupus, a disease in which the immune system attacks itself, so I was accustomed to health scares—but none like this. I hastily signed into the ICU and rushed to her room. I can still feel that chill of death that hovers in hospital hallways. It stilled my steps. I froze for a moment when I gripped the knob of her door, before gulping down courage and pushing into the room. I don't remember eating or drinking that day. All I could think was, *What is wrong with Mom?* And would her lupus make it worse?

Mom was lying in bed, eyes closed, seemingly unresponsive, and my heart stopped. My knees felt weak, as if every bit of strength I had was about to abandon me. I turned to my sister who was hugging herself, sobbing quietly. She'd been there all day and it was almost midnight. I got caught up on everything I'd missed, how they ended up there, what the doctors had said so far. Then, I sent her home to get some sleep.

My mother was in an induced coma. It turns out she was severely dehydrated and that she'd passed out outside the hospital, which is when the nurses were legally able to take her inside without her consent. There was blood all over her arms and clothes from her nosebleed. My phone was buzzing every few minutes with family members checking on how she was doing. Everyone seemed to think my mom was just having another really bad lupus flare. I put my phone on silent; I didn't want to speculate or read a bunch of texts that would further frustrate me. I was hurt, sad, and scared. I sat on the edge of her bed and rubbed her feet and nestled my hand inside of hers. Hours later, the doctor told me she had a seizure and her kidneys were failing. And she'd waited too long to seek medical attention.

"There's nothing we can do, I'm sorry," he said.

I sobbed until the ache in my chest couldn't churn any more tears from my eyes. They were puffy and swollen and bone dry. I sat there with her all night and all morning until my sister returned to relieve me. I went to a hotel to get a little sleep. My plan was to rest so I could fix all this tomorrow. Fix Mom. Somehow.

It had been a few weeks since the last time I saw my mom. And even then, I'd worried something with her was off. Zoe International had built solid name recognition in Houston on the event planning scene by then and I came into town to support a pop-up shop she was putting on. This was a pop-up shopping event that hundreds would be attending. Mom was a bit hard to reach leading up to the event, but I assumed it was because she was busy with last minute details. We agreed to meet at the event.

But when I showed up to the event my mom was being rolled around in a wheelchair. *A wheelchair!* Never in my life, even with all her lupus flares, had I ever seen her unable to walk safely. Her skin, which was usually lush and soft, was crinkled like paper that had been balled up and tossed away. Her golden-brown complexion, which used to shine, had paled with a grayish pallor. Her hair was pulled back into a messy ponytail, as if someone had roughly arranged it in a nightcap and whipped it off that morning without grabbing a brush. She was wearing basic sweats and a T-shirt with socks on her feet and slip-on Adidas shoes. I froze, staring, gawking at my mother across the crowd. People whispered as they passed, which I was used to seeing, but they weren't whispers of awe that usually surrounded my mother. It was a shock. I shouldered my way through the buzzing crowd and took over wheeling her out of her own event into a nearby shop and eventually home. My mom wasn't well.

I stayed in Houston as long as I could after the event and tried to get answers from my aunt. But no one knew when and how Mom's condition had gotten this bad. We all assumed it was somehow a complication from her lupus, but none of us were sure. And Mom played it all down.

"I'm fine. Would you mind getting me my robe?" she'd said before wrapping herself in the colorful silks of a kimono-style robe that used to make her look like some sort of goddess. On her then it looked like a curtain panel hung to hide a broken window. Before returning to LA, I made Mom promise to go to the doctor the next morning and keep me informed. She agreed.

A few weeks later, I got an eerily concerning phone call from her.

"Mammas?" She'd call me that sometimes.

I heard a voice yell, "Get on out of there now, come on!" A bang drummed on a door on the other end of the phone, punctuating the angry shouting voice.

"Is that Aunt Robin? Why is she yelling at you, Mom?"

"Oh, honey, it's—" Her voice broke off and she grunted in pain. My heart skipped a beat as panic set in. She wasn't telling me everything.

"Put Aunt Robin on the phone," I ordered in a tone that left no room for argument. My mom reluctantly let my aunt into the bathroom and passed her the phone. Aunt Robin updated me on the previous eight hours.

My mom had been on the toilet all day. She kept saying she was going to go any moment. But for some reason she couldn't. My aunt's voice was strained with frustration and fear. I tried to talk my mom off the toilet but wasn't successful. Eventually she fell asleep on the toilet and my aunt dragged her to bed. The next day is when I got the call from my sister outside of the hospital.

Seeing how swiftly things had declined with my mom in just a few weeks shook me up. There I was, building a fashion empire in Los Angeles, focusing on and developing my marketing strategy and designs. My business was thriving in a way I hadn't even conceived was possible. Everything new that I tried worked because by then I knew what made my customers click ADD TO CART. I intimately understood how my now millions of followers could be turned into customers, which days were best to post online, and how to orient my website to drive traffic to the items I wanted site visitors to consider first. My skills as an entrepreneurial fashion brand were razor-sharp. I knew what I was doing and that translated to rapidly growing success. I was on top of my career. And being on top meant Mom didn't want for anything.

But here she was struggling with something I could not fix: her health.

Her life was unraveling. And the most frustrating part was that I didn't fully understand what was wrong. Neither did my sister or my aunt. We just knew that Zoe hadn't been feeling well for a while and hadn't been telling us the full truth of what was wrong. What would another six months do to her? Would she even have that long?

I refused to roll the dice and find out.

I was in Houston with nothing but my phone and laptop. No clothes, toiletries, nothing. But I decided right then to stay in Houston for as long as it took. The doctors might be out of answers and solutions, but I wasn't.

What proceeded was six months of living between my mother's hospital bedside in Houston and popping back to LA for quick-turnaround trips only when absolutely needed. But in those six months, her health continued to decline. Helping my mother felt impossible. Everything else felt pointless. My business didn't ring with the excitement it once had. I was a hollow body going through the motions when my assistant would call me and I'd tell her what items to prep. I couldn't design, despite how much I tried, so I just coasted on previous items that sold well. I didn't care about Babes. I didn't care about anything. My mother was dying! And there was nothing I could do about it.

My first trip back to LA is when things really began to decline. I didn't want to leave, but I needed to get a few things from home to be better prepared for staying in Houston for an undetermined amount of time. When I returned, my mother had a severe bedsore on her backside and was on a breathing tube because she could no longer breathe on her own. Over the next few months, she'd whittled down to seventy-four pounds. She is five foot seven.

Eventually, the breathing tube was removed. But she wouldn't eat. She was going through psychosis from the heavy meds and wasn't herself anymore. Turns out that at the pop-up show earlier that year she was already experiencing some symptoms of psychosis. There were weeks in that hospital where she didn't know who my sister or I was. She would hallucinate and seem stuck in time. They attached a feeding tube to her eventually to force nutrition, but in her hazy mental state, she'd pull that out. So they cuffed her to the bed. Everything just seemed to go from bad to impossibly worse. And somehow the following day, *even* worse.

Staring at my mother every day was like watching a film with sped-up time. She'd transformed so much and was almost unrecognizable, which only sank me further into depression and hopelessness. Early into her stay, the doctors tried to do surgery on her intestines since she hadn't been able to go to the bathroom.

My mother was a slender size two or four. But as she lay in bed with a swollen stomach and face, she appeared six months pregnant.

There were moments where she'd seem better, and she'd move from the ICU floor to a lower floor. But then she'd decline again and be rushed back up to ICU and usually into surgery for something. And yet I sat there every day waiting on something more promising from the medical experts. But nothing reassuring ever came. I wanted to pull out my hair because I didn't know *how* to figure this out. I didn't know *how* to do anything to improve Mom's health. I was entirely out of my lane. My ability to help my mom, to hold her up during this time, as she'd held me up time and time again as a kid with what little she had, was nonexistent.

There's nothing I can do, I remember thinking. In those few months drowning in depression, I cried more than I spoke. Mom was at the end of her rope, and no amount of my working harder or paying for things or being innovative was going to save her.

The hospital became more than my home and work office. In many ways, it was my prison. I couldn't imagine what life was outside of the hospital. I'd forgotten what it felt like to hope. I was stubborn, so I never stopped coming to the hospital and sitting with her. But I'd lost the ability to picture her life any other way.

Until one day Mom was rushed back to the ICU with internal bleeding.

By then I'd read her charts a hundred times. Anytime the nurses changed her medicine or dosages, I knew the amounts and drug names. This particular day, the doctors were talking to one another instead of me. Concern was dug into their brows as they ordered the nurses to check Mom's vitals again, run another blood panel.

"What's wrong?" I asked, putting myself in front of the main doctor giving orders.

He looked at me then his eyes darted away. He sighed.

"Tell me."

"We can't stop the bleeding. She's just in really bad shape. We're going to try everything we can, but you should begin making arrangements in case things don't go the way we want."

"No!" I yelled at him.

He didn't even flinch. He just walked past me back to Mom's bed and kept going. Time and motion seemed out of balance. My head swam. They told me when they admitted her that her kidneys were failing and there was little they could do. And we'd lasted seven months so far! The hope that I thought had abandoned me unfurled itself in my chest, fighting for life. Mom could get past this, too. They were wrong. But Mom lay in bed unconscious for the rest of the day. Her gums paled.

That night I refused to go to the hotel. I'd come from nothing and built a wildly successful business. I knew how to make much out of small odds. I didn't build a seven-figure business because I knew everything about the fashion industry or even how to run a small business. I built it by putting one determined foot in front of the other to learn every facet of retail, social media marketing, and anything else that became related to my business. My capacity to succeed with Babes wasn't limited by the parameters of what I already knew. It was determined by what I was willing to hunt down and find out. Could that apply to my mom's health as well? I felt completely inept relying on the doctors' explanations of things. If there was any hope for my mother, Google and I were going to find it.

I stayed up all night on my fifth coffee reading up on medication. My sister and I printed out the side effects of every medication my mom was on and reviewed all of them, paying close attention to the ones that had side effects that could exacerbate internal bleeding from the ulcers she'd developed from being on so much Tylenol. She was on over ten medications, so it took hours. But several rabbit holes later, We found one medicine with side effects that seemed concerning. It was for her anxiety, and it appeared it could be intersecting adversely with her laundry list of medications. I checked my list of scribbled notes to make sure I had the right drug. I dashed into the hall.

"Nurse!" Breathless, I showed her what I found and asked about that specific drug. Her face scrunched in shock. Within minutes she ordered the other nurses to take my mother off the medicine. Over the next few days, Mom's internal bleeding gradually improved.

We'd saved her life.

From that point forward, I double-checked everything the doctors did. I researched every medicine. I made them consult me before deciding anything. And they listened because they didn't want a lawsuit on their hands. I did extensive research on every single decision they approached me with.

A few weeks later, while I was back in LA for a few days, I got a phone call and didn't recognize the voice. It sounded like Elmo. It was my mom. She'd had a breathing tube in so long, her vocal cords were still adjusting. It was sort of unsettling but brought me so much joy. This was the first time I'd heard her talk in months.

"What's up mammas? What have you been up to?"

I just laughed.

<hr />

My mother's health is still in flux, but she is living in Los Angeles with me now and has a good quality of life. She's able to visit, have dinner with my sister and me. She is healthy, even if just for now.

I look back on that season and I'm stilled by how building Babes proved to me that I am capable of literally anything I'm committed to accomplishing. And how I'd almost forgotten that when my mom was sick. We often forget we possess this "super-power" when faced with something very emotional and scary. Fear can be stifling. I'd almost given up until I remembered how I'd built my business with nothing but a poverty-ridden childhood on my back—by teaching myself all the things I didn't know. And by standing firm in the face of the seemingly impossible. Both things I am able to do because growing up on the outside equipped me to be an obstacle-scaling go-getter.

In that season of helping my mom by doing my own research and accepting that I can accomplish anything, I switched from a fixed mindset to a growth mindset, an idea presented by the brilliant Carol Dweck. I (and the knowledge I possess) am not inherently "unchangeable." To accept that would imply that we are stuck as this version of ourselves. I rejected that as a child, and I reject that now. And you should reject it, too. I believe that we undergo change when we give our full effort. In those hospital months, I learned all I could about lupus, kidney failure, long-term hospitalizations, intersections of complicated drugs, and all manner of other things I had no idea about before 2019. My potential wasn't bound by what I already knew but by what I was committed to learning. I didn't have to already know how to balance a budget or run a profit and loss statement to build Babes. However, I learned it all with dedicated self-study because I can learn anything. It reminded me of the job search rejections I kept getting in Houston, then LA. They were looking for résumé experience proving what I had already learned instead of looking at the capacity and potential of what I could learn. And they missed out. Because I am an asset.

After this season, I approached my business—and my life—with a newfound confidence. I'd built a business from literally nothing and I'd saved my mom's life. I felt like I could do anything. I must point out, of course, that we cannot control everything that's thrown our way in life, *especially* devastating health diagnoses like this. If I hadn't found those conflicting drugs and my mother continued to progress poorly, that would not have been my fault. The idea here is not to take blame or amend whose responsibility it is to fix a problem that crops up. Because problems, especially health problems, are sometimes not fixable. The idea is instead to reframe how we view our own capacity to do *some*thing about the situation in front of us. Keeping in mind that our efforts cannot guarantee a certain result, we can still do everything within our power to steer things in the most positive direction possible. I wanted to give my mom every single chance she had. That's all we can do (and that's a lot!). There are some things within your control in situations like these, even when it seems like so much is not. Try to focus on that.

Resist the idea that your plateau of knowledge has cemented and you know only what you know. I say this especially to my fellow lady outsiders. That's not how brains work, girl. Get out there and fill that head with some more. Especially when you're faced with a mountain that feels unscalable. Become an expert in nutrition to revolutionize your chances at beating cancer. Digest the pages and pages of research on cutting-edge AI-based technology used to enrich classrooms—to transform bare bones, low-budget classrooms into globally competitive academic environments. Steep yourself in the latest fashion fad and where its designs fall short and find your niche.

Mom's health scare was a sage reminder that the goal isn't to arrive, it's to keep evolving.

Read, study, learn, evolve. And repeat.

THE OUTSIDE SCOOP

I Refused to Do Nothing

I often feel like things are out of my control because, well, they are. When I find myself in these situations, what eats at me the most is feeling like I'm just sitting, waiting for the situation to resolve itself. I consider myself a *doer*. I like to get things accomplished. I live for that dopamine rush I get when I cross things off my daily to-do list, which is why when life tosses me some circumstances where my hands feel tied, I often feel momentarily overwhelmed and defeated. I've found myself in this situation time and time again: when I was on Stacy's couch, when I was in Houston but couldn't find a job, when my mom was sick. But in each situation, I found that doing *some*thing felt better than doing nothing. This was a habit I'd formed, in hindsight, built out of sheer stubbornness. I refused to do nothing. I would do whatever I could with what I had. That mentality galvanized me in college when I was determined to never be poor again. And it carried me through every hard season in my life.

Getting around the wall in your head that says *There is nothing I can do* is a feat in itself. When I'm in that place, first I must recognize that I'm in that headspace. Then I consider what needs to happen. If my brain is very fuzzy because a situation is particularly stressful, I'll make a list of everything that, from my point of view, needs to happen. Then I sift through which of those things I'm capable of trying. (I'm a list person, can you tell?) Other times, I explore possibilities in conversations with trusted friends because one of the best ways to get out of my own head is to literally get my thoughts out of my brain. Going to someone outside of myself offers a fresh perspective because they can often see my situation and my ability to impact it from a vantage point that I do not have.

As you look at an impossible circumstance you're facing professionally or personally, what is *something* you can do? It doesn't matter if it's the smallest action you can take, just take it. You'll feel better and usually gain some momentum to do the next small something, too.

9

Exploit the System, Guilt Free

AFFIRMATION

I will not feel guilty for leveling the playing field

The first time I was called "nigger" I was walking down Hollywood Boulevard.

It was 2012. I was twenty-three years old. Of course, I knew racism existed long before that. That instance of name-calling was just another reminder. But one of the most shocking reminders of just *how* racist the world is happened on May 25, 2020. At the time, everything already felt like it was upside down, being in the middle of a global pandemic. Then suddenly it was on fire.

I was flipping channels during lockdown, restricted from leaving my Los Angeles home. A news headline scrolled across my screen, and I froze.

SHOCKING VIDEO SHOWS KILLING
OF UNARMED BLACK MAN

A deep, hardened sense of dread pinned me to my seat. I still remember the way it felt when I read those words. Like ice was clawing its way up my spine. It wasn't the first headline I'd seen like that. I didn't believe it would be the last. I turned off the TV immediately and swiped on my phone instead. I didn't want to see another video. I didn't want to see another Black person lose their life at the hands of senseless violence. But later that day, a still image of a police officer's knee crushed against George Floyd's neck, pinning him to the pavement, flashed on my phone while I was scrolling social media. My grip tightened. A lump rose in my throat. Suddenly I couldn't look away. It was broad daylight, there were tons of bystanders. I didn't see any guns. So I pressed play and watched.

My breath stuck in my chest as I watched George gasp for his own. It weighed on me like an anchor. The grip on my phone slacked and I hugged myself, curling up in a ball on my couch. I watched every single second of that video, frozen with shock, fear, pain, and something else I didn't have words for until later—hopelessness. That day, I couldn't shield my eyes from the ugly, disgusting truth—that four hundred years later, it felt like Black people's right to humanity had to be earned.

The image of George's face pressed against concrete charred my memory, stained the back of my eyelids. I did not sleep without seeing his face, without hearing him call out for his mother as death inched closer. The police officer's stoic coldness at his plea for mercy. The disregard of basic humanity. Without wanting to, I replayed the images of George losing his life over and over and over in my head. George's face would sometimes morph into another in my memory. Ahmaud. Breonna. Trayvon. But it always ended the same—with death.

I didn't talk for the rest of that day. Not to anyone, by voice or text. Then reports came out about George's use of drugs and crimes he'd committed in the past, as if any of that is justification for being suffocated on a street, unarmed, with an audience of powerless people watching. I felt trapped. I felt hopeless. Is this what my Black children will be dealing with if I have them? Did I want to even bring them into this world where they have to prove their humanity?

My business seemed so insignificant at the time. My sales were steady—the world was on fire, but my customers were still shopping. I didn't have the emotional bandwidth to dream up any creative launches or even work. I had launched a line earlier in May, so my inventory was full and there were items I could sell. But each day felt hollow, as if several would blur into one. I didn't want to work. And apart from when Mom was sick, I always wanted to work. About a week later, I logged onto social media and there were black squares everywhere. People were posting black squares in solidarity for our community under the hashtag #BlackoutTuesday. I remember finding it oddly perplexing but was also being moved by how many were participating. It was an odd mix of emotions where in my heart I ached to see justice, but my subconscious whispered that this is all our community would get—black squares. So I should find satisfaction in it. I participated and shared a black square, but it never satisfied. It never made it feel better. But it was something and I was so desperate to *do* something. For most of us Black Americans, every day for several months was like waking up in a never-ending nightmare. White pride was at an all-time high. The racists were no longer hiding and it got really scary. But, on the other hand, white guilt was clearly visible.

Then, suddenly, the #BlackLivesMatter hashtag began to trend and the world seemed to shift. The focus was no longer just on George, but on all Black people, our oppressive history with America, and spotlighted the successes we've had. I remember thinking, *Of course our lives matter.* It was sad that this needed to be proclaimed so boldly. The next few weeks were full of people advocating for shopping at Black-owned businesses. More and more Instagram profiles showed up with hashtags that businesses could use to identify as Black-owned. I eyed my profile on Instagram, which didn't say anything about my race or ethnicity. I considered the tag, shifting uncomfortably in my seat. I perused a handful of my colleagues' pages and they'd all attached the tag to their profiles. I even saw a few white entrepreneurs and people in the industry who were urging their followers to "not shop their sites" and to instead support a business that was Black-owned.

But my finger still hovered over the profile edit button on my page. I couldn't do it.

I tossed my phone aside and took a walk that first day of seeing this new trend. Over the next several days, I saw so many social media stories and posts with images of piles of packages and business owners thanking everyone for "all the sales." There is a Black-owned coffee shop down the street from my house, and when I walked my dog Marley one morning, the line was around the building. That was a first. Starbucks, also on that same road, was a ghost town, as Yelp and Uber Eats had even added a Black-owned section listing restaurants where patrons could support our community. My boyfriend, Donte, and I waited in line for two hours at one of them. The world was supporting Black businesses in a way it never had before. It seemed money was being made in abundance everywhere in our community. Everyone I knew who was Black was proudly waving their arms saying, *Shop here!* Except me.

How did all the money flooding into our community fix what happened to George? How did it help his family? If I was going to promote anything, I wanted it to be about lasting change, not myself. A week into this moment, my sales were still steady despite not having the label. And to be clear, my being Black was not a secret. My regulars knew if they followed my business or personal page. I am not shy about it. I was designing T-shirts and hats with Black-empowerment messages on them long before 2020. I eyed my profile on Instagram, which *still* didn't say anything about my race or ethnicity in the bio section. Again, my finger hovered over the tag. But I swallowed and closed the app. I couldn't do it for two reasons.

First, it felt icky. Labeling myself as Black-owned, right then, felt like taking advantage of a tragic situation. I felt guilty profiting in the aftermath of someone's very public, very inhumane, death.

Second, I am a Black woman with my own perspective based on my personal experience. Would I be profiled by a police officer the same way as others? Absolutely not, and that's the world we live in. Racism is disgusting. Colorism is, too. Both are realities I can't ignore. I felt weird about it. I felt like I didn't deserve to be wrapped up in this moment because of the advantages I have experienced in my life. My sales were great and I walked around the world with little fear from the police. Why did I deserve anything out of this tragedy?

I never told anyone how I was feeling. I just kept my thoughts to myself and continued supporting Black businesses—as I always had before May 25, 2020. But every time I opened Instagram, I'd think about adding the tag, then my insides would wriggle, nauseating me, and I'd swipe to look at something else.

I was fortunate that Babes was running itself. But I did wonder if I was making the right decision and questions churned in my head.

Was it poor timing to declare myself as a Black-owned business on Instagram?

Of course I feel like I've been treated unfairly, but was this my opportunity for advancement?

With Babes doing so well, was I being greedy?

The other side of my brain argued back—but I do deserve support. I am a part of this unjust system. As I wrestled with these impossible questions and memories I wished I could forget, I was reminded of the first time I realized that the world wasn't fair.

―――

"Stop all that talking and listen," Ms. Derbin, my seventh-grade history teacher, said.

She was hovering near the front of the classroom, trying to quiet the buzz of chatter about the upcoming weekend. There was a movie everyone was excited about opening that night and no one was interested in listening to Ms. Derbin remind us about our test on Monday. Or at least that's why I thought no one was listening. I hooked my hands in my lap and kept my eyes on Ms. Derbin. My seat was in the front of the classroom. And I'd been studying all week for the test she was about to remind us about.

"Look at your notes on the Reconstruction era—"

The bell buzzed and my friends rushed into the hall. I gathered my things, said goodbye to Ms. Derbin, and joined my friends in the hallway.

"Are you going to Edwards tonight?" Edwards was a theater in southwest Houston. And of course I wasn't. With what money? I also knew I should probably study a bit more. This test was an end-of-semester grade. My teachers always went on and on about how straight As would "open all kinds of doors" for me when I finished school. I liked the sound of that, so I studied hard. I always sat in the front of my classes. I turned in every bit of extra credit work available. I had straight As, and I intended to keep them.

"I'm not," I said. "Plus, I need to study."

"Girl, hush." Tenisha roped her arm in mine, and I realized she was trying to discreetly slip a rolled-up piece of paper into my jacket.

"What is—"

"*Sssh*. Be cool."

I shouldered my way through the bustling crowd and found a corner of the hallway, pulling out the paper for a better look. Tenisha hovered over my shoulder, a smirk playing on her lips.

"What is this?" But I knew the minute I asked. This was a copy of Monday's test questions and all the answers. "Where did you get this?"

Her brow scrunched. She pursed her lips and snatched the paper back. "Why?"

I shrugged. I don't know why that occurred to me. But I wasn't going to get caught up in trouble. How did she know that was even the *right* test?

"Do you want a copy or not?"

"Nah, I'm not getting in trouble."

She laughed. "Your loss. Everybody has a copy."

"Is that going to look suspicious if everyone gets an A?"

"*Or* it'll look like the test was really easy."

I still wasn't convinced. I liked getting things right on my own. I would earn my As the right way. Tenisha and I walked to class, and neither she nor any of my other friends mentioned anything about the test again.

Monday was test day, and I slid into my desk in Ms. Derbin's class and pulled out two pencils. I set them perfectly parallel to the edge of my desk along with my pink eraser. I popped my knuckles; I was ready. Ms. Derbin handed me my test with a smile. For a moment I thought about saying something. Nerves sloshed in my stomach. No, I wasn't going to snitch. People who break the rules get in trouble. That's how it worked. Momma always said that. Policemen always said that. The people at church always said that. I slipped on my sweater and got to work.

Two days later when Ms. Derbin handed back the tests, my heart thumped in my chest as she approached. The test was not easy. I actually had to guess on a couple of the questions. The paper slid across my desk with a red number circled at the top: 94.

"*Yes!*"

I looked over at Tenisha who was getting her test back as well. Her smile split in a grin, and I spotted the 98 at the top of her paper. My heart skipped a beat and my jaw dropped.

"You got a 98?!" My yell garnered stares. I looked around and every paper I spotted from my vantage point at the front of the room was 90 something. Tenisha winked. I felt sick. When class was over, I rushed into the hall. Tenisha and a few others were calling my name. But I didn't want to talk. They cheated and aced the test. They didn't even get in trouble! I put in the work. They didn't. And yet we reaped the same reward. Tenisha and the rest of my classmates never got in trouble. I, on the other hand, spent the rest of the day annoyed.

What I understand now is that it's common for people not to put in the work and yet reap the reward. That's life. That's people. That's capitalism. That's America. The founding economics of this country were set up to allow those in power to reap rewards while building on the back of others who actually *did* the work. Why did I grow up poor? Because my mother was poor. And she was poor because her ancestors were poor. They were poor because . . . *yeah.* My great-great-great grandfather was a white man who owned slaves. He died in 1879, but his legacy lived on. In some records I've found, he was likely French nobility. Whether or not he was an aristocrat, he was well-off, a landowner. And his fortune, everything he owned, probably passed down to his white, legal children.

Not the bastard children of the slaves he raped—my ancestors.

Capitalism in this country was designed on the exploitation of certain groups of people, and that wealth disparity has rippled throughout time.

I stewed on the questions tugging at me again with a new-found clarity.

My ancestors were slaves. My light skin wasn't something I

picked out of a magic box for myself. The fair skin of my genetics is a source of privilege in this backward country. But it is also a bitter reminder of the fear and terror under which my great-great-great grandmother brought my mixed-race ancestor into this world. I would not feel guilty for any of that.

The system in which I'd built my livelihood was never designed to protect, uplift, or propel me—or any Black person—toward success. It was designed to build *its* position at the expense of Black people. My people. *Me*. My boyfriend drives a luxury vehicle. He's been pulled over multiple times in Beverly Hills on suspicion of his car being stolen. Once, this ignorant situation almost made him late to work. His supervisor didn't make a big deal of it. But what if they had? What if they'd reprimanded or fired him for being late? Where would that have left him? The more questions that occurred to me, the more my jaw ticked. When merely *existing* and trying to build success clash, that is a problem. And it is not just with my boyfriend. Or me.

It is systemic.

Feeling worthy is what I realized I was struggling with. I felt as if I didn't deserve to take advantage of a moment where other business owners were being spotlighted. The truth stabbed me like a knife between the ribs. The system that puts obstacles in my way, then denies the existence of those obstacles, did not get to make *me* feel unworthy. Because one, this moment of opportunity would pass. Eventually the world would move on and the plight of the Black American would no longer be a headline or hashtag. Because oppressive systems are buoyant. They will rise to the top.

They will do whatever they need to do to reassert themselves as superior. Look at history.

And two, I am owed something the system will never give: a fair chance at success on a level playing field.

I was done feeling guilty about making a system work for me that was designed to work against me. An opportunity had presented itself. I was in a position to take some of my power back, level up, and shine. So, I did.

First, I added the Black-owned tag to my Instagram bio. Next, I researched a list of websites that were looking for Black businesses to highlight. I also adjusted my landing page to feature my empowerment collection from 2018, bringing it to the forefront of my website. The collection was a series of ball caps and socks with an embroidered fist on them. These always sold well to my customers and existed well before this BLM moment America was having. When I published my site with the new items and looked over my social media profile, with the tiny "Black-owned" tag under my business name, I bit my lip. *Would I regret this?* Less than a week later, I had my answer.

On June 19, 2020, I threw a "party" at my house. Parties then, in a pandemic, were sort of like three or four people sitting outside in lawn chairs shouting at each other from six feet apart. My apartment was in the shape of the letter U with a courtyard in the middle. So I invited some friends over to celebrate Juneteenth. Suddenly, someone screamed. And my first thought was, *Oh lord, what did y'all break?* But my sister ran toward me, her red wine sloshing in her hands.

"What is it?"

"Look!" She shoved her phone in my face. Beyoncé—*the* Beyoncé—had shared a photo on her website of my leisure maxi dress as a part of her Black parade promotion, recommending Black-owned brands to shop. Underneath the dress was my company's name in black letters.

The world spun.

I fell into a nearby lounge chair, and someone put a drink in my hand. Tears burned my cheeks, and I realized I was crying. Beyoncé was promoting *my* business?! I was so glad at that moment I'd added the Black-owned tag on Instagram and put my name on those lists. The momentum continued and the second half of 2020 was my highest-selling period. I was making roughly five figures in sales a day. And that Black Friday I made $87,000 in a *single* day, the most I'd earned in a twenty-four-hour period ever. I was floored. If we had always been supported like this, perhaps I wouldn't have been so opportunistic about it at the time. But this was a trend that for many was rooted in the emotion of the moment. It wouldn't last. But while it did, I took what I could and never regretted it.

Find and exploit opportunities in systems designed to hold you down. If you're in the minority, you have less power than those who outnumber you. The system was structured to keep you in your place. To keep Black people in their place. To keep women in their place. The system is not going to *give* you equal footing on *any*thing.

You have to take it.

THE OUTSIDE SCOOP

I Got Really Good at Being Painfully Honest with Myself

As my eyes began to open up to more opportunities for how I could exploit the system to get ahead, I had to spend intentional time unpacking the source of my hesitance. I had spent a long time convincing myself that I had enough wealth and opportunity relative to other people. That I didn't deserve to get more than I already had. I squirmed in my seat as words like *greedy, selfish*, and *privileged* floated through my consciousness. But I realized when I'm weighed down by the urge to just be thankful to have *any* opportunity at all in a system that historically eats people like me and spits them out, that is not guilt. That is a trauma response. And I refuse to give that control over my actions.

My knee-jerk reaction was to dress up "guilt" as something else. Boiling the immediate reasons my brain gives me down to their core motivation took practice. The key was learning to be very honest with myself to suss out the core of my hesitation, of what's really holding me back. Even when it is painful. (Especially when it is painful.) Now, as I search my heart on making decisions such as these, if I find that guilt is at the core, I ask myself two questions: One, does this action harm anyone? And two, does it break any laws? If the answers are both no, I do it.

What systems exist in your life that do not serve or help you but instead put more obstacles in your way? How can you exploit cracks in those systems for your own gain and to level the playing field for yourself and people like you? What are you allowing guilt to hold you back from?

10

Let Trauma
Be a Motivator

AFFIRMATION

*I will use my past
to build my future*

My phone is always in my hand whether I'm in the bathroom or steering the Tesla. But one unassuming morning in spring 2021, I began to wonder if being glued to my phone is an actual problem. It's just sort of the way the world works now. That day I was awakened, as I am each day, by the sound of my goldendoodle's paws padding the wood floor. My stomach gurgled. But before stepping out of bed, I turned on my side and grabbed my phone. I tapped my lock code, my thumb panned across my screen to the Shopify app, moving in its practiced rhythm.

"Sup," Donte said, getting out of bed to let the furball out to potty. I heard him but didn't respond, fully absorbed in the spinning wheel icon loading my business's sales portal. I sat up in bed as the wheel kept spinning.

"Is something wrong with the internet?"

"Internet's just fine."

Finally, after what felt like hours, the screen loaded. My eyes snapped to the big black number at the top: *Sales: $700.* I exhaled.

This was my morning routine every day since launching Babes. By early spring 2021, I was consistently making around $2,500–$3,500 gross per day. The day wore on and I checked my sales again—after breakfast, every time I sat on the toilet that morning, at lunch, and five or six more times before bed. Nerves welled up in my chest as tight as a knot each time the screen loaded. At bedtime that night, Donte reached for the light at our bedside. I was checking my sales for the very last time.

"You're stressing yourself out doing that all day," he said.

I lay awake stewing on his comment, thinking about why my sales app was such a regular part of my day. The answer was obvious at first—I'm a business owner. I should be in the loop on how my business is doing at any given point. But that was only half of the truth. The other half I'd pushed to the back of my mind. But that night, there was no escaping what was driving me to keep compulsively checking my sales app—the memories of growing up without a steady roof over my head. I relived one moment over and over until I fell asleep: the night I realized Mom's Jeep Cherokee was where we had to live.

In ninth grade, when I was fifteen, my mom was singing at a swanky nightclub and lounge in Houston. We were still living in a corner of the studio space that her friend was renting. But when Mom started dating Jack, the owner of the high-profile bar, he set us up with an apartment in River Oaks, the ritzy part of Houston proper. Think Beverly Hills or Fifth Avenue. That vibe. Yes, he moved us *there*. And it was furnished! My sister and I had our own rooms. Mom would pick us up from school in her rusted red jeep and we'd park in our reserved parking spot between all the fancy cars. It felt like our days of hopping around from friends' couches were finally over. It was like living a dream.

But one Saturday morning, Mom shook me awake in a panic.

"Get your stuff, now." She tossed a bag at me as I wiped the crust from my eyes. My sister was moving around already.

"What's wrong?"

"We have to leave, Ciera." Her lips thinned; her gaze fell to the floor. "Quickly, please. I'll explain when we get in the car."

"Like . . . leave? Forever?"

She looked at me and said nothing. But I could read the strained lines in her face. We were leaving this place like all the others before it. I stopped with the questions and did as Mom asked while she paced in the living room on the phone. I chewed the inside of my lip and dug my toe into the carpet. We'd had to leave places before, but never so suddenly. We'd only been at this apartment for two months. Usually, when we were on a friend's couch or air mattress, Mom would tell us she found a new place and there would be a future date when we'd move in. Eventually we would have to leave that place, but she'd always explain it as if she'd found a new place that was better or cheaper or closer to her work. This time felt different.

I forced myself to start packing my stuff, dusting off and putting my chess trophies and medals in my suitcase. I always did that first. Once I was done, I sat with my sister on the couch.

"What happened?" I nudged her with my elbow. She shrugged; her eyes glazed with tears. But I didn't have to wonder much longer. As I peeked in the fridge for something to assuage my rumbling tummy, I passed by a letter unfolded on the counter. At the top in big black letters were two words: EVICTION NOTICE.

Once we'd filled our bags with as much as we could, we loaded them into the trunk of Mom's car. The apartment was full of stuff we couldn't take because we didn't have room in the jeep or enough time to make multiple trips. We had to go *right then*. My mom drove us out of the apartment complex gate. And we drove. And drove. And drove. It was a Saturday and Mom didn't have any gigs to attend. She was silent for most of the drive, and I suspected she was crying. But she never turned so I could see her face.

When the sun had gone down, she pulled the car into the top floor of a parking garage. We looked out at the Houston city skyline.

"Are we almost there?" I asked her, yawning. Wherever we were going this time, I was eager to get there.

"Try to get some sleep." She rubbed my arm, tucking her bottom lip. I could tell by the sag in her shoulders, the dull look in her green eyes, that there were so many words hanging on them that she wasn't saying.

I realized we weren't driving anywhere else. This random parking lot was our destination. We didn't have anywhere to go.

A lump welled in my throat. I broke Mom's gaze and instead looked out the window at the big city with so many buildings, so many people. Houston's downtown is full of mid- and high-rise buildings, condos, apartments. I'd never felt more different, more like an outsider, in my entire life than I did in that moment. I imagined that behind each rectangular pane of glass in those towering buildings was a family, all tucked in for bed. Safe and sound.

I watched as lights turned off one by one, the darkness of night deepening, and pulled my jacket tight to my chin, wishing I was in one of those buildings, behind those panes of glass. In one of the many homes with my own walls and bed. Eventually I fell asleep.

That was the first night that home became Mom's car.

The day after Donte got me thinking about my habitual sales-checking, when I woke up in the comfort of my Los Angeles home, which I owned, I tried really hard to not touch my phone upon waking up. Honestly, part of my motivation was just proving my boyfriend wrong, because isn't that what great girlfriends do? I dragged myself to the coffee pot with one eye open. Two sliced avocados were there as well as a matcha latte with almond milk, my favorite way to liven up a humdrum midweek day. (The boyfriend-of-the-year award goes to Donte, clearly.)

As the magical wake-up juice steamed in the cup, my fingers instinctively patted my pockets, then the counter, for my phone. I tightened my hand into a fist, reminding myself of my plan. I could wait to check my sales; I could stave off the worry and fear until I made it to the office in a couple of hours. I could sit here and have breakfast with my boyfriend and be present. I deserved that. He probably did, too.

We ate. I ended up checking my sales at a traffic light on the way to the office because it was taking too long to actually get to work. But that patience was solid progress for me. The red light finally turned green, and I made it in way later than I'd planned.

(LA traffic is ri-damn-diculous.) I walked inside with the long-ago day we were evicted still churning in my mind. And I just had to stop and admire the state of my office. My assistant was already there, along with a few others, preparing to pack inventory. Packages ready for mailing were stacked in neat rows. The printer was spitting out labels.

"Busy night," my assistant Teresa said. "It's going to be a long day today."

I smiled. A long day meant a profitable day. I thanked her, handed her the Starbucks I'd picked up for her on the way into work, and settled at my desk.

My business was running like a well-oiled machine.

I built this.

From nothing.

How I'd built all this kindled in my mind. I was stilled, standing there in the doorway as I recalled how Babes started with ten dollars in my pocket. How when I was ready to list items online for sale because I was poor, I found a *free* place to do that to minimize my out-of-pocket expenses. When I saw that social media—another free resource—could be a powerful tool to engage directly with my customer base, I dove in, aggressively building a platform for social selling. As money began to flood into my business, I cut coupons, budget shopped, and continued to look for ways to snip costs, no matter how much money I made.

All because I was terrified . . . I *am* terrified . . . of being poor again.

My past traumas motivate my present-day hustle.

Teresa knocked at my door, then came in.

"A return." She set a bag on my desk. Next to it was a hand-scribbled note. I love hearing *why* my customers return things.

"Need more breast support for something like this."

The customer was one I knew well. She was full-figured, thicker in the middle than in the hips. The top she returned was a tube top with thin straps. If this top didn't work for her, it didn't work for more than her. She may be the only customer who took the time to send in a return, but I always assume one voice represents several. And if there was a subset of customers that it wasn't working for, that was a problem for me. I hated wasting products. But I hated disappointing customers more.

"Send her an email to thank her and issue a full refund. And bring me one of these tops in my size, please."

Teresa did. I turned the top in my hands, tugging on it to assess its amount of stretch. A more fitted top would help hold itself up. This fabric had good stretch, but the straps were thin. I chewed my lip. Then, with practiced precision, my brain began picturing ways this top could be reworked inexpensively to give it more support. Determined not to waste anything. I put on the top and moved both straps to one shoulder. The entire fit changed from loose on my bust to tight and supported. This could work. I spent the rest of the day designing an alternative shirt made from the same design that wasn't working for that customer. No restitching was needed, so redesign costs were literally zero. I let Teresa know we'd compile the inventory that was left over once this collection ran its course and rephotograph it showing the versatile ways it could be worn. Because it was a redesign, we could do the reshoot casually in the office, with the staff, without hiring models or a professional photographer. *Another zero-cost shift.*

"Bitch, you're brilliant," Teresa said.

I laughed. I don't know if I'm brilliant or just resourceful. As I sat there, pulling the to-date numbers for that shirt's sales, I realized rectifying this customer's issue was an instinct I had *because* wasting things as a child wasn't an option. When you don't have a lot, you cannot afford to waste it. I'd dealt with shelter and food insecurity as a child, which left lasting impacts on the person and businesswoman I am today. However, I've figured out a way to churn those anxious penny-pinching habits, such as the resistance to wasting *any*thing, and my obsession with being aware of my sales, into habits that kept a tight bottom line for Babes, enabling it to succeed. My million-dollar business started with a thrifted outfit from a clothing resale shop that I hand sewed.

I am perpetually and subconsciously worried that one day I'll come home to boxes and a move-out notice, house keys I am forced to hand over. That fear hugs me like a scarf tied around my neck too tightly. It steals my sleep in the middle of the night at times, and it spikes my blood pressure from time to time. That same fear of being broke has shaped how I manage my business fiscally and has massively contributed to its success. As much as the fear of being broke still haunts me, I also appreciate it is responsible for all I've created. I am miles ahead of so many other small-business owners *because* I was poor.

I was convinced I was the only poor fashionista from Houston with nothing and no one in Los Angeles. (Not true.) I just *knew* that there weren't others bumming it on couches like I was. (There are *tons*.) I may have been the only woman, and curvy woman at that, trying to break into the stick-figure-obsessed fashion industry in a major way, but there were millions of fashion lovers wishing for the same things I did. The voice in your head telling you *I'm the only one who feels this way* is a liar. Treat it as such.

Often we are tempted to assume we are alone in our trauma. As outsiders, we sometimes *expect* to be ostracized and are often surprised when we are not, in fact, in the minority. I can tell you confidently that you are not alone in your trauma or disadvantages. It might feel that way because you're keeping it all bottled up and letting silence isolate you. Not opening up to yourself or others about this experience and not digging through it to find what's there besides the pain and scars don't help you in the long run. I *know* this is not easy. But this practice of silence keeps us in bondage to our trauma. There is too much power in unearthing your trauma and reflecting on what you learned and how it's made you stronger to not do the work. When you work through it, your lenses have a different prescription, so to speak. You can see the world differently. *Use* that vision!

The woman partner in the type-A, male-dominated C-suite can see the sexist remarks, the lecherous side-eyes, the misogynistic microaggressions for what they are—fruit of insecure men— because she's soared past hundreds like them to get to partner. She is confident, unfazed, and laser-focused on what she wants, whether it's the CEO spot or to oust some of her male counter-parts. She has survived worse than those men. She's faced up to her difficulties. And she's armed and equipped to keep running circles around them because those difficulties and the trauma she's suffered now motivate her. As outsiders, we are often hard-wired to be resilient in the face of obstacles, which can be unfath-omable to those who have never known the adversity of existing in the margins.

The point? The marks left from my traumatic past are not all scars.

And neither are yours.

So let your trauma be a motivator instead.

I want to be very careful not to minimize the damaging effects of trauma. There are ways my childhood has truly scarred me that are not helpful at all. Dealing with your trauma, be it on your own or with a licensed and trained professional, could be transformative for you. Most important, be kind to yourself, practice lots of self-care, and be patient. Unpacking trauma is heavy and can take many failed attempts and much support to get through.

Facing your trauma will not erase your scars, but it could help you realize that not *all* the marks left on you are scars. Maybe you see them as armor that keeps you safe, tools you employ in your everyday life, or unique ways of understanding the world. You might think differently because of what you've been through. You might notice skills that you have that others lack (such as my penny-pinching tendencies) because of experiences you'd like to forget. Wherever you are on your journey to reflect on your past traumas, never forget that you are more than the sum of your past experiences. You are a gold mine of potential.

Use the past that you'd like to forget to shape the future you're determined to have.

And always remember: take care of yourself first.

⸺

I don't know how long we lived in Mom's jeep. It's a bit hazy. But it was for a large portion of that school year, so I'm guessing at least several months. Long enough to be seared in my memory as something I don't want to endure again. But just because it wasn't an ideal circumstance doesn't mean it was inherently unhelpful. I learned to do a lot with a little. I learned how to pivot quickly and repurpose anything. If a car could be a house, a tube top could definitely be a skirt. You get what I mean? I don't look begrudgingly at my years of living in a vehicle. I instead look at what I learned from that phase of my life. This is an intentional and active choice I make to take ownership of the lens I choose to view who I am, where I've come from, and what I'm capable of. And in my experience, seeing the gems in our experiences is far more motivating, productive, and inspiring than not!

If digging around in your past to unearth gems is too triggering, take a beat to focus on healing. Then come back a bit later and try again. That's what I did.

THE OUTSIDE SCOOP

I Sat with My Trauma

I dealt with a lot growing up that I'd like to forget. As I worked through my experiences over the years, I did what I like to call "sitting" with my trauma. I did not approach it as something to fix. I cannot fix my trauma. I've already told you it cannot be erased. But what I could do was allow myself to feel it by sitting with it in small doses. I could not do this all at once. I had to do this over the course of ten or more years. I'm still doing this. Sitting takes the pressure off having an objective in mind when I open the boxes of my past I'd like to forget. If I am bogged down with how I should feel when I sift through my past, how I should be over it by now, how I should have learned a particular lesson by now, et cetera, I can leave these box-opening sessions feeling defeated. When examining trauma is involved, feeling defeated is a slippery slide to spiraling. To guard myself against that, I just sit with my past with zero expectations or goals of what I need to do. The very act of opening "the box" of my past and rummaging around inside is the only thing I commit to doing. I take items from the box one at a time and look at them from various angles. And when the box gets too heavy, I close it back up and plan to come back to it another time. Each time I return to this box it is lighter because I've been gradually taking things out of it and looking at them. Again, I recommend doing this alongside a licensed therapist. But it is amazing how much lighter some areas of my past feel now that I've unpacked a few boxes. Writing this book is clearing out a whole host of boxes, and I hope it might help you clear out some old boxes, too. But there are definitely some boxes that I am not ready to open. And that's okay. I can come back to that closet another day. So can you.

I Forced Myself to Consider the Positive

As I sat with experiences from my past, my mind would wander to how they've affected me. When I sit and just let my mind wander, I find ties between habits, response patterns, and preferences that I have now because of something that happened in my past. For example, I have a collection of designer tennis shoes. Walls of them. Collector's editions. It's kind of an obsession. It took me years to realize this was a trauma response because I could never buy the real ones as a kid. But it's not a damaging one. What I learned about that shoe collection is it demonstrates that I like to celebrate the things I have overcome. I am proud that I am now able to fully indulge my love of shoes, because I've overcome a lot of adversity to be able to do that, and that isn't an inherently bad thing. Dare I say—it's positive. This seemingly small act opened my eyes to the value of celebrating small wins.

When I first began sitting with my trauma, I made a list of the not-so-great ways my past was shaping my current behavior. It wasn't very obvious at first, but the more I'd search, the clearer it would become. For example, I realized that growing up without much made me very stubborn when I want something. I churned that into resilience, which has been critical in thriving as an entrepreneur. As a child, so much of my life was out of control. Now I crave control. I am using that desire to fuel my motivation for learning about new things. When I founded Babes, I delved into studying the intricacies of retail business ownership, such as photography, lighting, and editing; tax structures; and so much more. The more I knew, the better I could control the evolution of my business. I've unearthed so many gems by using my trauma to drive me where I want to go.

What gems are buried in the trauma of your past? What could you gain by committing to unearthing them?

This "Past in the Present" list is a compilation of realities from my past and how they have shaped my habits and mindset today. Here's mine in case it helps inform yours.

1. I did not have a lot of material things growing up ➤ I can be stubborn when I want to buy something I really like.

2. I did not have a consistent home ➤ I will live in a nice place, no matter what.

3. The men in my mother's life weren't reliable for stability long-term ➤ I refuse to depend on a partner for anything.

4. I had a lot of experiences as a child where a circumstance would end poorly for me or my family ➤ I expect things to go wrong or blow up or end negatively for me.

5. My childhood was filled with hustle energy, watching my mother try to make ends meet ➤ I don't know how to not work or truly relax.

What's the first thing on your Past in the Present list?

11

Embrace Failure

AFFIRMATION

*I will survive my worst failures
and be better because of them*

One morning in 2021, I grabbed my phone, rubbed the crust from my eyes, and the big black number of my total sales for the previous twelve hours was a single digit.

Zero.

My brows smooshed together in indignant confusion at the big black zero on the sales app. I rolled my eyes and tossed it aside. Technology could be so unreliable. I dragged myself to get a cup of coffee and eventually went to my computer to try the sales page there. But it said the same thing. Since 6:00 p.m. the previous day, not a single purchase was made on my site. *My sales portal must be down*, I thought to myself. My simmering irritation rose to a boil as I threw on clothes and headed for the office. By the time I arrived at my work desk, my sales page still said zero dollars. It had been fifteen hours since the last transaction. This sort of glitch was a first. At this point in 2021, my page received an average of ten transactions per hour every single day of the week, around the clock.

So, I decided to dig a little deeper and reach out to customer service for the sales software I use. After a fifteen-minute wait, they confirmed that no one else using their program had reported having issues. There was no issue on their end.

My sales portal wasn't broken. It was accurate.

The truth slapped me so hard I fell into my desk chair. Over a now sixteen-hour period, I had made *zero sales* for the first time in Babes's history. My world came to a screeching halt.

If people weren't buying, there had to be a reason. Perhaps I could rework the latest collection I'd launched? I swiped through my sales history on my most recent collection—a series of off-the-shoulder maxi dresses in bright colors. They'd sold decently well. But was reworking a launch I *just* marketed a prudent choice? I wasn't sure. I wracked my brain the entire drive home.

Eighteen hours. Still no sales.

This is like a slow, torturous death to a small business owner. Once home, I texted my staff and told them to take the day off. There was no point in paying them to be there when there was no selling happening.

"Is everything okay?" my assistant asked when she called me.

"It'll be fine. Just take the day."

"Will I still get paid for the full day?" she said, her voice strained. "I need the hours."

I sighed. "For today, yes, I'll pay you. But wait to hear from me about the rest of this week, please. I'm sure everything is okay. I just need to . . . figure out some things."

"Ciera?"

"I'm sorry, T. I have to go. I'll call you back." I hung up on my assistant, guilt knotting my insides. In my rational brain, had I stopped to really think, I would have realized that no sales for one day didn't mean I'd need to start letting people go. But my lived reality is that when my money is adversely impacted in any substantial way, my body physiologically responds with panic, stress, and worry. Upon later reflection, I realized self-doubt and imposter syndrome were also at play. I thought my falling sales were an indication that the jig was up. That I'd rode the wave of success and it'd finally come to an end because for me riding the high wave of success can't possibly last. It took me a while to realize it, but this fear was rooted in a feeling that I didn't belong at the top, which is something marginalized people feel all too keenly. Often marginalized people like me feel "just grateful to be here" rather than a true sense of belonging, believing that they will eventually be discovered and ousted. It took me several years to unpack why it is so easy for me to believe that my success won't last. I am still unpacking it. But at that time, I understood none of this. My mind snapped into a trauma response before I could even entertain the reason.

I cleaned my house top to bottom, trying to figure out what prompted this sudden shift in sales. But by bedtime, I had no more answers or ideas of how to get out of this mess than I did that morning.

An entire week passed, and my sales didn't change much. And I hadn't told a soul. Not my assistant. Not my boyfriend. None of my friends. If I didn't discuss it and I'm able to fix it somehow, did it even happen? If I didn't discuss it . . . I wasn't a failure to anyone but myself. I'd brought in about $800 gross, not profit, in a span of the last seven days. I was used to bringing in that amount in the first *hour* of a day.

Donte was on his way out one afternoon in the blur of the days that week and I was in sweatpants that I'd worn for I don't know how long. Plates filled with leftover *cooked* food—because eating out was a thing of the past—were all over the house. I couldn't remember the last time I'd left my house or slept more than a few hours at night. My staff had been blowing up my phone every day that week wondering what was going on. He stood in the doorway, eyeing me warily.

"You all right?" he asked.

"I'm fine!"

"Clearly." He kissed me and minutes later the front door closed. Suddenly assaulted by the stench coming from my armpits, I got in the shower, turned the water as hot as it could go, and sobbed. My worst nightmare had occurred. My business was failing. And just like that I felt like I was sixteen all over again, sliding into Mom's rusted Cherokee.

Three weeks later, Babes had earned only $3,000 the entire month. And that wasn't profit. That was not nearly enough to cover my office rent, inventory, website fees, and other business expenses. Forget about my personal expenses such as the mortgage, utilities, and car. It was really happening. My business was falling apart, and I, too, was unraveling. I sat there for a while then muttered to myself, "You're in trouble." I knew it in my heart before I ever let it come out of my mouth. I couldn't even tell the man that I lay in bed with every night, that I share every part of myself with. This was the one thing I struggled to share with anyone because I wasn't ready to face it myself.

The moment I said the words aloud, something in me shifted, like a drain finally coming unclogged. First, I texted my sister:

"Can you talk? I'm not okay." Then, I sent an email to my financial advisory team requesting a meeting. I needed to know if I was in dire straits. That night, for the first time in a month, I actually slept through the night.

The meeting with my advisers came two days later. I folded my arms as the team of faces who were used to seeing an entirely different Ciera appeared on screen.

"Good to see you, again, Ciera," my lead planner said. "How have you been?"

I gave an obligatory smile, struggling to look directly at them, embarrassed it took me over a month to even set up this call.

"Can we get started? How bad does it look?" *Will I survive this?*

My lead planner started his presentation of the numbers he pulled for my business the last five weeks. After ten minutes of long-winded explanation, I couldn't hold my tongue anymore.

"So what do you recommend?" *How do I fix this?* I wanted to ask. *How do I start making money again?* But I kept my desperate thoughts to myself. They couldn't tell me why my site wasn't being shopped as it used to. It was my job to figure that out.

"The reality is, Ciera, is that retail is just slow right now," he said. "We're seeing this across clients. And don't get me started on inflation." He smiled and I scowled. "This dip in sales isn't your fault." He smiled again.

"Right," I muttered. An excuse is what he was giving. I don't like excuses. The market not doing well was one I almost let stop me before. And then a New Year's Eve party shattered everything I thought I knew about the retail market during this time of year.

In December 2017, my friend had a holiday shindig at Soho House, a members-only club. When I got dressed for the party, I'd planned to wear a dress that had a plunge neckline and a pair of red bottoms. But it was unseasonably cold outside for LA, so I slid into a pair of my boyfriend's joggers with a crop top. And some comfy boots to complete the look. I sort of looked like I'd dressed up in gym wear, but I was cute.

"You look good," my friend Lana said when I walked into the party. *Did I?* I wondered. Donte's joggers were baggy on me, so they fit more loosely than my own. I wore them scrunched at the ankle.

"I like being comfortable," I told her as I sized up everyone else in the room. To my shock, just about everyone at the party had a similar idea. I saw comfy leggings and hoodies dressed up with sparkly tennis shoes or heels. There were some in oversized T-shirts tied with a belt at the waist. Lana, my friend, was in leggings and a cropped hoodie with cute boots and fun socks.

"So no glam this year apparently," I said.

"Girl, everyone is cold and tired. It's been a *year*. We just want to chill."

I laughed. I felt that. As we celebrated the holiday season and end of the year, that night stuck with me. I hadn't considered how the end of the year is full of activities and places to go. And after it all, I just wanted to come home and curl up on my couch in a blanket with a big cup of cocoa. An idea nudged me. Loungewear was in, clearly. Glamorous clothes weren't the mood.

This was an opportunity.

A week later, I was at the door of my favorite supplier in the fashion district the minute the clock struck opening hour. It was January 2 and businesses were *just* opening back up, and like me, many were expecting an initial rush of customers buying discounted sale items, then bleeding into a snail-slow month. January was always a slow month for retail. No new lines, just selling off stock of unwanted inventory at a discount. January in many ways was a month off. As a business owner, I'd save up to "survive January," not expecting to make much money that month. The excuse was *the market*. The door didn't unlock, and it was three minutes past opening time, so I rapped on the door a bit too eagerly, her door chime jangling.

"Ciera?" The door finally opened and my main manufacturer Jenna's eyebrows rose in genuine surprise. "Is the spring stuff ready already?" Jenna wasn't used to seeing me this early in the year. But people were shopping *some*where and I intended to make it Babes.

"Not spring. I want to see what you have on hand for now. I'm going to do a comfy line."

"When?"

"Next week."

To her I'm sure my idea made zero sense. No one put out lines in January. I knew that. There were plenty of excuses not to try. But I am not one for excuses. The market may not be ripe for it. But the oddly cooler weather, the exhausting year, and that post-holiday fatigue was the *perfect* time for a collection that emphasized comfort. Speaking to the moment was a clever idea.

Jenna and I worked around the clock to get samples prepared. I practically lived in her store for days. By the second Friday of January, I had an inventory of Babes joggers ready to photograph. I did a simple warehouse shoot and launched the following Monday. That jogger collection ended up being my bestselling January ever. In a typical January I'd make around $30,000 and profit very little, if any at all. Whereas in a typical month the rest of the year, I'd make around $100,000 and profit a fair amount. But in January 2018, I brought in just under six figures.

After that, I pinned a phrase to the top of my computer: focus on where the money *is* being spent. And from that season forward I filtered each idea for collections through that lens. The market is never going to be in my control, but that doesn't mean doing nothing is the answer. I had to focus on what I could control and play into the market. That was the key to surviving any low-selling season when it comes.

In this dire moment in 2021 when my sales had never been lower, that's what I had to do again.

I pulled my sales records for the last six months. At that time, money was also being spent on comfortable clothes being dressed up, a trend from the pandemic that had stuck. I wanted to see where the very few sales I *was* getting were coming from. After a few hours of analyzing, it was very clear that 1) new customers were discovering Babes for the first time and 2) the pieces that were selling were my basic pieces, which I launched when Babes started.

The next morning, I pulled everything that fell into the "basic" category and counted inventory. I had quite a bit on hand, but I hadn't promoted these pieces in *years* because my regulars knew about them. And I hadn't even *thought* about new customers. I had been focused on putting out fresh new content for existing customers. But the data was clear: I needed to switch my focus. New customers were finding my brand every day. I'd grown complacent, assuming my customers, new and old, knew about my bestsellers: items like the yoga tummy control legging, the Babe turtleneck, and the racer tank.

I called Teresa. "I have a plan." I could hear an expulsion of relief on the other end of the phone.

Anyone can ride the wave of success, but when things come to a screeching halt is where the rubber meets the road. That's when *lasting* success flounders or is forged. If you find yourself in this situation—whether a new product you put out failed, or a presentation you did at work flopped, or your performance toward your personal goals has been falling for a while—first, admit when you're in trouble, to yourself and to others. (It's very likely the people around you already know it.) And second, don't use the climate around you as an excuse. Reflect on your actions, what you've been doing or not doing, gather as much data as you can about what's been going wrong, and then start to work on a solution. In my case, I had to look at where money was being spent and find a way to connect (or reconnect) with that.

With my sales in the garbage, I needed to do something quick. But I couldn't wrap my head around what that something was until I looked my failure in the face and learned from it. This season is one I think back to often because it's a vivid reminder of what happens when my back is against the wall. I pivot, I adapt, I thrive. Not because all my efforts are destined to succeed, but because I have accepted that failure is coming and I will scale that obstacle as I have every other one. My perspective on failing now is simple: I will survive and be better because of it. Simply put, you have to embrace failure to overcome it.

THE OUTSIDE SCOOP

I Recognized I Could Only Improve from Here

Failure was a hard pill for me to swallow because it felt so final. But once I failed, a tiny voice in my head was like, "Okay, what now?" I'd already failed. I knew what *not* to do, which is half the battle. In my business it felt like I was at the absolute bottom (or very close to it). And that's when it hit me—if I'm at the bottom, the only place to go is *up*. That paradigm shift when I messed up reanchored me to focus on solutions instead of more problems. It contextualized the past as the past and the future as something with positive potential. And that fueled my motivation and creative thinking. As a person who is wired to constantly see the ways things can go wrong, it takes very intentional effort to 1) set my mind on solutions and 2) believe that upward progress is still possible.

Are you that way, too? How does your self-perception shift when you think about failing? Do you take failure too personally? Can you see beyond past failures you've had? Try making a list of ways you've failed in the past, using bullet points to highlight some ways you were better after those experiences. In what areas of your life can you expect bumps in the road? Can you brainstorm things you might learn from some of those potential experiences so you're ready for them when they come?

12

Reject the Fear of Losing Power

AFFIRMATION

I have a power that cannot be taken away

I was kidnapped when I was three years old.

That experience left its mark on me in ways I couldn't really unravel until the 2021 season when my business felt like it was falling apart at the seams. After facing my failures and brainstorming solutions, I created a plan to fix it: produce a line that speaks to the moment of the market and target new customers. But I couldn't do that by myself. My struggle to embrace failure and admit Babes was in trouble wasn't the only realization that came out of that season of my business. I also learned that I don't like asking for help. But as I sat at my desk after another long day of trying to fix my sales, I realized the smartest way to give my next line its best chance was to do just that. And it felt like the biggest pill to swallow.

My stomach sloshed at the idea of actually picking up the phone or typing out that awkward text to tell my entrepreneurial colleagues and friends what was going on with Babes.

"Why haven't you asked?" my boyfriend asked a few nights after I'd decided what I needed to do.

"Because—" But I stopped. I wasn't sure what the answer was. *Why couldn't I ask for help?* was the resounding question playing in my head for the rest of the night. My shoulders knotted with a distinct sense of foreboding. I had always hated relying on others. As I searched myself and my past for answers, I realized it all stemmed back to me seeing how powerless my mother was in her relationships as I was growing up. And there was one experience that seemed to capture it all.

———

My parents met in a small town in Texas. She was a senior in high school. He was seven years older. After a few years of dating (and two kids later) they'd split up. Over the years, I've heard multiple versions from family members of how my father took me from my mother without permission and kept me away from her for *months*. The precise details of what happened and what was said have been lost to time and age. But traumatic events like these leave fingerprints. I've gathered those, reflected on what I can recall, and pieced together what I imagined happened from the various accounts I've heard. Let me paint a picture for you.

One day, while watching me so that my mother could work, Richard, my biological father, took me to his place and refused to return me to my mother. At first my mother tried to give it time. But eventually she realized my father wouldn't be reasoned with. She tried, for several months, to talk him into returning me. To let her see me. (My mother had limited recourse since he is legally my father.)

Until the day he called her, threatening to drive off a bridge.

"I'm gonna do it, Nancy," my mom remembers him saying.

She recalls him threatening violence previously so she didn't take his words as empty. She was terrified. She told me she cried so long and so hard her eyes ran dry. But her body still wept, tearlessly. After that moment, she recalls that she heard nothing for several hours. I have faint wisps of memories from this time and the one thing I remember vividly is this burning ache to see my mom. But it didn't matter. He was in control. He had all the power. And he made me, and my mother, believe we had none.

In my nightmares I always imagined some heroic person overhearing his conversation and stepping in to snatch me away from him. But that's apparently how it did happen.

My uncle, my mother's brother, called my mother after word of Richard's threat somehow reached him. He told her that he was willing and ready to help her get me back however he could. So one morning, when my father least suspected it, my uncle grabbed me, slipped out of the house with a blanket over my body, and met my mother blocks away.

I remember it was frigidly cold outside. But as soon as I saw my mom standing next to a small red car, I instantly felt warm. She fell to her knees, opened her arms, and I flew into them. My mother had been working for months to get me back, but each prior attempt had failed. This time her extraction plan worked, and I never saw that small town again.

My mother left her entire life in that tiny Texas town after that day. She left the family members she relied on to watch me during work, the village of people the old proverb refers to. That town was where my dad was. And my dad wasn't safe. So my mother made the decision to leave. But the life that followed for my single mother was not easy. There is a power in having a stable foundation, whether it is self-made or a compilation of aunties, uncles, and grandmothers. When my mother left that small town in Texas, and the partner she'd hoped to build a life with, with two young children and nothing to stand on, her power—her stability—hung in the balance.

How then could a mother model having that sort of power to her two impressionable daughters? She couldn't. As I've talked about throughout this book, what proceeded after that horrid day was a string of various living arrangements. In early elementary school, we lived in a trailer owned by a friend. Despite my mom fleeing an abusive relationship with very few resources, she had a beautiful voice and she was a hard worker. At one point she sang backup for the R&B icon Patti LaBelle. Three years later, my mom moved us to Houston to be closer to our grandfather. More connections meant more stability, more power. We moved into an apartment and Ron, a guy Mom was dating at the time, paid the rent. One day Ron and I were in the car, and he was dropping me off at karate. Mom had to work, but Ron was stepping in and was the only healthy version of a coparent I'd known. The world felt centered on its axis. Like it would never fall off again or tip over. As Ron helped me tie on the white belt to my uniform, he turned to me and said, "I'm thinking of asking your mother to marry me. What do you think about that?"

Spoiler alert—they never married. As a kid I wasn't in the weeds of why they fell out. But the fact remained when he was gone, I felt his absence. The apartment he'd gotten for us was gone, too. After that relationship, my mom moved my younger sister and me about every twelve to eighteen months. I went to a different school every year of elementary school. By seventh grade, we'd secured a low-cost living situation in an old commercially used warehouse.

In addition to singing, my mom had begun organizing community events under the name Zoe International. One morning at that warehouse housing, I'd rolled on my side and the weight of the air in our mattress under me dipped. My sister rolled into me, her slick skin sticky against my back. It wasn't exactly a room, but it was fairly private, a wedge of about an eight-foot-by-six-foot space where my B2K poster of J-Boog and my sister's of Lil' Fizz grinned down at us. It was Saturday, which usually meant tagging along with Mom on jobs, grabbing free food at various community events. I wondered what we were going to do that day. I rummaged through a plastic bin of one of those little cubby-style storage cabinets for some jeans. But I shimmied a little too hard and my collection of chess trophies and medals from elementary school tumbled to the floor. I set them back exactly as they were.

"Mammas, you're up?" Mom asked, poking her head around the divider.

"What are we doing today?"

"Surprise!" She handed me a white shirt with *Zoe International* on it in black cursive. "Today's event is going to feature . . . *me*." She beamed. Beside her name on the tee was her face.

I gasped.

This was it. I just knew it. We had *finally* made it. No more air mattresses for much longer. This event was at the Miller Outdoor

Theatre. Their events were usually advertised on the radio. Sometimes the news! This was going to be a huge event.

And it was.

Thousands came to hear Mom sing. Mom's brand grew tremendously after that event. She booked more event jobs. She met more people who could help her climb the success ladder. But no matter how much Mom's star seemed to rise, our lives didn't change.

After living at the warehouse, Mom dated Jack, a local business tycoon who set us up in the fancy apartment that only lasted two months. Mom eventually found someone else after Jack to help with our living situation. But they always left. We always gave the keys back. And as I mentioned before, for part of high school, "home" was Mom's Jeep Cherokee.

When I think back on that particular season of being picked up from school in a home on wheels, what I remember most is the pride my mother wore, content that in the face of everything at least she was able to give her daughters some sense of a home that wouldn't be taken away. Her car was more dependable than the relationships she was accustomed to relying on.

My mother had power that was taken away. I watched her fight to take it back her entire life. And I lived my life in fear of the same thing happening to me.

She relied on others to provide stability for us my entire childhood. What I saw as a kid was that our security was wrapped up in someone else keeping their word to her, in their feelings for my mother and us not changing. And I watched as this blew up in our faces time and time again. And it all started with Richard. If the person who is responsible for half of my genetic makeup can't be relied on, how could anyone? I vowed to myself to never be in this sort of situation.

One day, I would have power.

And no one would take it away because I'd never rely on anyone.

That fear of losing power would never hug my shoulders again. The only person I could trust was myself. It was that reliance on myself that pushed me to find a way to get off of Stacy's couch when I first moved to LA. It was that resolve that kept me innovation-focused through the pandemic and strategic during the BLM "moment" of 2020. So it was annoyingly inconvenient that now, years later, I needed to abandon this practice of self-reliance to get out of a debilitating financial rut.

I told myself that night in 2021, after procrastinating on reaching out to my peers, that I would do it first thing the following morning. I was going to ask for help, but somehow do it *without* giving up my power.

The following day I reached out to a list of contacts with a short and sober explanation: Babes was not doing well for reasons I hadn't sussed out yet. And I needed their help. Specifically, I asked them to boost my collections on their platforms to their audiences. This was a big ask. I was asking them to essentially share their audience with me. I clicked send on the first email and bit my nail. Nerves wriggled in my tummy. *Please let this work.*

Where my mom had erred, I realized, was that she relied completely on others for stability. And it gave them leverage over her stability. The people she relied on had full access to her sense of stability—her power. Ron, Jack, and so on could take it away with the snap of their fingers. And they did, often. Sometimes because the relationship ended. Other times because their own financial situations had changed. I would watch my mother collect bits of her power back and start piecing it together, piecing our sense of stability together, as she settled into another seemingly promising relationship. But the whole puzzle would suddenly crumble between her fingers. Because she wasn't building stability on a foundation that was *hers*.

That would not be me, I told myself as I hit send again. I was now on message number three. It got a bit easier with each explanation. My business wasn't flourishing, but it was still a business I could build on. It had its own power in that alone. My mom was sharing her power with others. She did that more often than building her own. Reaching out for support in my case was different because the power I built still existed. I was going to ask fellow designers to share their power with me without giving up any of my own. There's a subtle difference between the two.

When I rely on someone, I risk giving up agency over my power. But there is a difference between relying on someone and asking someone for help. If others in my industry would share their audience with me to help my collection reach a wider audience, I could use the benefits of their power without giving up any of mine.

━━

That night the truth hit me like a ton of bricks: seeking out and accepting help didn't have to rob me of power.

Often, we outsiders get used to doing things for ourselves, to being lone wolves, learning to depend on only ourselves. This made me very bad at asking for help. There is strength in doing things on our own because it's within our control. But this can lead us to become isolationists because that preserves a sense of self-power. And when we are able to grab hold of this sort of power, we are not quick to let it go.

It then feels almost unnatural to ask for help and goes against everything we've told ourselves. In my circumstance, the stakes were high. I was used to having to work hard to get ahead. Being on the outside in a battle for power is like a cure for complacency. But I needed support this time. I therefore had to find a way to get it without making myself feel powerless.

Everyone responded enthusiastically. Their posting about my company and sharing their audiences with me was just the boost I needed. I found an entirely new swath of customers. They snatched up my bestsellers, which were now featured prominently on my site, in addition to selling out my travel-inspired line. One person I'd reached out to mentioned that her business was in the dumps as well at the time and she'd been too chicken to reach out for help. We were commiserating over lattes a few weeks later when I reopened my sales app and the big black number was finally back in the four digits.

Babes was back!

Help is part of growing and evolving. No one does anything alone, no matter how self-sufficient they may appear. Half the stuff you see on the internet, especially social media, is posturing. Beware of drowning your dreams of success in the ocean of your fears. You are not a powerless no one. You are someone, and as long as you hold on to your power firmly with your two hands, no one can take it unless you give it to them. And when the time comes to ask for help—because there will be a time when you will need others to come alongside you—seek a way for them to share their power without giving away all of yours. If you've built a foundation to stand on, *stand* on it!

The kidnapping was a traumatic event and the first time I'd experienced my own and my mom's helplessness. But looking back, it is a vivid reminder that I am not that scared little girl anymore. I am a woman with my own business and power. And I don't need to be afraid of losing this power, because no one can take it from me unless I *give* it to them.

THE OUTSIDE SCOOP

I Was Selective in *Who* I Asked

When I sat down to decide who to ask for help, I was very selective in who I chose. I reached out to people who I'd helped before or people who I have the ability to help in the future. I didn't want to create an imbalance where someone would feel as if I owed them something. I kept the list focused and intentional. There was no benefit in asking people for help who couldn't realistically help me. I was careful with where I opened myself up to be vulnerable to ensure the potential gain was there.

I Was Methodical with *How* I Asked

I wanted to avoid getting a "no" when I asked for help. So I made sure to ask for simple help that would not consume a lot of someone's time or resources. For example, I asked for them to share a post on social media with a link. Or accept a collaborative post on IG. I avoided rejection because it was an easy ask. I also prefaced my request with the assurance that asking for help would not be a regular thing. I never wanted anyone to feel like I was opening the door to continually bleeding their resources. Instead, I was up front about my situation, direct and clear about what I was asking for. And I made sure to say what I was willing to offer in return. I was honest about what I was not willing to do, both to avoid any confusion and to ensure I didn't give up more of myself than I wanted to.

Asking for help sucks. I get it. But it's inevitable, so finding ways to do it that make you comfortable is a good idea. Can you practice asking for help in small ways? Perhaps low-stakes situations are a better place to start than asking for help with big life things? Or the inverse of that might be more comfortable for you. Regardless, spend some intentional time considering ways in which you *could* ask for help that don't make your skin crawl.

When considering how to share in other people's power without giving up your own, identify the critical areas where you need help, whether it's boosting your retail business on social media or securing free childcare so you can fully devote yourself to a hobby that you're passionate about without denting your budget. Focus on the areas where you need the most help. You don't need to ask for everything you need, just the most important things. If you need more social media exposure, can you ask five peers with moderate followings to boost you in addition to the one friend with the massive following? Can you or are you willing to return the favor if they ask? Would you agree if you were in their shoes? If not, how can you sweeten or soften the offer? If you need help in more than one area, can you allocate different asks to different people so you're not asking too much of one person?

13

Be Uncomfortable

almost had an anxiety attack while signing the closing docu-
ments on my first home purchase.

When you are used to being poor, going through hundreds of
pages of disclosures about what you're going to pay, and for how
long, and to whom, and red-tape this and scary-regulation that, is
*stress*ful. I'd never committed to anything so serious in my entire
life. But in 2020, as the closing team pushed the final paper my
way, a small crowd hovered nearby with glasses bubbling over
with champagne. I dragged the *s* of my last name out longer than
I needed until I finally worked up the courage to set the pen down
on the table and hand over the last signed piece.

I'd done it.

After living in my mother's car, on a borrowed couch, on a
blow-up mattress in a warehouse, on a springy mattress on a floor,
after home was an ever-elusive idea and not something I could
hold with my own two hands—I, Ciera Rogers, first of her fucking name, was a homeowner.

Reliving that day will never get old. Champagne was in my
hands; tears were in my eyes. I'd bitten off my own piece of this
country and I could call it *mine*. An asset that would be passed

down through generations, that would start a legacy of wealth that could be built upon. My home in northern Los Angeles was a three-bedroom house with a courtyard in the center. It was old and outdated with peeling paint. But in Los Angeles, this was a gold mine.

I stuck the key in the door and stepped inside with air held tight in my lungs. The click of the key in the lock, twisting in response to the rotation of my wrist, flared a heat in my chest like I'd never felt. It felt . . . powerful. I felt powerful. This home was mine. As I walked the house jotting down notes of all the things I wanted to change and customize, goosebumps danced up my arms. *I owned this.* And it all started with ten dollars and a dream on someone's couch. I put plans in motion to rip out the kitchen and living room walls to make the whole house more open concept. I also wanted to tear down the courtyard's interior walls and instead have them be an entire wall of accordion glass doors to really bring the outside in. I was going to lean into this home, making it everything I dreamed of. I deserved that.

With all my stuff still at my old place, that night I slept in my house on an air mattress, but for the first time in my life, I did so with a giant smile. The next morning, I headed back to my old apartment.

"Actually, let's pop into the office real quick," I said as my boyfriend and I zipped through morning traffic.

"You really want to go there now?" His lips screwed in a smile as he rerouted us toward my office. I don't know why he was so surprised. I was always at my office, checking in on inventory, keeping an eye on things. I was the epitome of a hands-on employer. Everything at the office was flowing as usual. My assistant was on top of admin and my other employees were packaging and going through their usual routine. As the clock ticked to lunch, I thought about what Donte said. I'd just hit a huge milestone the day before. I was a homeowner. And yet here I was, watching sales populate on my tracking page as if I was on Stacy's couch all over again waiting for my first outfits to sell. I bit my lip and fired off a text to Donte.

Lunch? I'm done.

My finger hovered over my screen . . .

Done for the week.

A week off wasn't so bad, I told myself. I'd earned that. I also had meetings with contractors scheduled to get the home renovations under way in the coming days. It was going to take two months, and I wanted to prepare those plans right away. I lunched outside at a gourmet sandwich place, and I remember the sun was really bright that day with a cool bite to the air. The perfect weather. For the perfect day. To celebrate what felt like my life aligning perfectly for the very first time.

That week I took off flew by, and I didn't miss being in the office. My assistant would call with questions from time to time, but that was all. Things ran smoothly and I decided to stretch that one week off to two, during which I turned my full attention to enjoying the fruits of my labor. I price-shopped for contractors.

Two weeks stretched into a month. I traveled, fell down a rabbit hole of interior design, shopped for furniture, floors, kitchen tiles, bathroom sinks, toilets. (There are so many kinds of toilets?! The one I ended up with has more buttons than my TV remote.) For the first time in my life, I spent mornings sitting outside, easing into my day, soaking up the sun, starting an exercise routine, and beginning to embrace the idea that I was no longer desperate to assure myself that I wouldn't be poor. As I walked through my house, surveying its many imperfections, the long way the contractors had to go, weeks on end of drilling sounds, hammers banging, sawing, none of it could steal the smile etched on my face. Just owning this house was making me money *daily.*

I did stop into the office from time to time during those months, but never the warehouse, which is where my inventory moves in and out. I'd check out any notes my assistant left for me on my desk, fart around on the computer, and leave shortly after. It's like one day I woke up and realized life could finally be about more than just work. I'd never imagined something like that before. It was completely outside of my paradigm. I, a Black woman in *this* country, from dire poverty, an outsider in so many ways, had earned the freedom to actually live. I realized I'd been living in survival mode for so long. I didn't realize until that season that there was more to life than work. And it was a beautiful thing. I began to daydream about working less, trips I could take, and ways I could step into this idea of doing more in my life than work.

Three months passed.

Construction was still in progress on my house. The two-month renovation project turned into five, and it was looking like even finishing by then would be a miracle. I was still living like I'd loosened the belt on my pants, the way you do after you've gorged yourself on a delicious dinner. And everything with Babes was fine. Until one day, six months after I'd closed on my house, my phone rang.

"Uhhh, so . . ." It was my assistant. "A customer is demanding all the money back she's spent here the last several months. She's spewing all kinds of stuff on IG. Not sure what to do."

Don't panic, I thought to myself. I'd dealt with my share of disgruntled customers. That's just part of business. And my approach is really unique, I think. Because my brand is so me-forward on social media, I end up interacting with a lot of my customers personally. I recognize a lot of my loyal customers' names. I know who regularly boosts my posts and engages online thoughtfully. But I hadn't really been paying attention to my social media those six months either. I had my assistant scheduling posts with captions I'd prewritten. But beyond that, I wasn't as into the customer-facing part of my business as usual.

When I arrived at the office, piles of inventory lay along the floor, waiting to be packaged and shipped out. This wasn't terribly concerning, but I did have a warehouse with plenty of space. I walked to the warehouse and peered inside where I found my employees and my assistant pacing.

"Teresa?"

"You're here, thank goodness. Okay, so . . ." Teresa proceeded to update me on this customer's issue with a pair of pants she'd bought. She handed them to me, then a whole pile of other, obviously well-worn clothes. I couldn't quite wrap my head around someone wanting to return the last several things she bought from me.

"There is also this." She handed me a folded note written hastily. "She sent it with the clothes."

This isn't flattering on my apple-shape, at all.
Babes usually does me better than that.
I'm very disappointed.

—*Tanya*

I pulled up my sales portal on my computer and sorted by this customer's purchases. She'd bought thousands of dollars in pieces from me over the years. She was definitely loyal. I opened my IG to some wild number of unread messages and comments. I'd missed so much. I'd *been* missing so much. I swiped past all of it and looked for her name. I knew this customer well if it was who I thought it was. She'd added her IG handle to her note. Sure enough, I pulled up her page and recognized her profile pic. Her latest post was her modeling the pants she'd just sent back. The caption sent my heart racing: "I made this look decent, but I had to get it tailored just to make it fit halfway right."

The date on the post was three months ago. And it was hearted—I'd double tapped it mindlessly because I guess I was scrolling so fast and just saw my pants and really didn't pay attention to the caption. I sank deeper into my office chair. I was so disengaged because I was letting out a breath for the first time in my life. I'd stopped paying attention to the ins and outs of the everyday. On some level I began to mangle the concept of work-life balance with being completely unplugged. That *that's* the defining indicator of success, the ability to be less hands-on and do more living than working. And while a piece of that may be true, the prevailing truth I realized that day is that the goal of building something successful cannot be to get comfortable.

I hadn't forgotten how to design. But my customer had picked up on my commitment to the company and my waning attention to detail. The shock of that stilled me. It was a sobering reminder of how quickly everything I'd built could unravel if I continued to not pay attention. This customer who loved Babes was determined to get my attention, and she had. (This is why I love my customers, by the way. The ones who have grown with the company and been there since the beginning really love watching it thrive. They know my brand well and hold me to it. I have the best customers!) At that moment, however, I was equally appreciative and frustrated.

As Teresa and I went to my warehouse to check out the inventory of this item Tanya had a problem with, I opened the door to a swath of disarray. Piles of a popular pant I sold were on the floor in stacks beside spools of thread, and my seamstress (I had one on staff now) was working on a pair of them.

"What are you doing to those pants?" I asked.

"I'm adding a slit to the leg."

I grabbed the pair and held it to myself. The slit she was adding was on the inside of the leg. Who puts a slit on the inside?!

"This is wrong!"

My seamstress's eyes widened.

Teresa bit her lip. "Uhhh, we've been sending these out with an inside slit since the line launched three months ago."

In that moment, it felt like watching myself outside of my own body in some kind of slow-motion horror flick. I could not be hearing what I was hearing. Teresa blinked, tears in her eyes.

"I'm sorry, I thought—"

"This isn't your fault," I said. "It's mine. One of many." What *else* had gone wrong?!

Fortunately, my customers loved the pants with the inside slit. None had complained. But I, the designer, strongly preferred it on the outside. That was the vision. When we restocked the line we offered the pants with the slit on the outside, and my customers loved them as well. It wasn't a big deal to them, but to me it felt like the earth had shifted on its axis. Something so seemingly minor could be catastrophic if I'd done nothing. Between Tanya's determination to get my attention and these pants, I was shaken to my core. I'd grown entirely too comfortable. And I didn't get to where I was by being comfortable. I got there by paying attention.

My taking a breath, leaning into a comfortable lifestyle, had bled into complacency. I'd passively assumed "making it" meant I'd reach a point where I was more hands-off and just collecting income. That's not real. I had to achieve balance—not work so hard that I burned out because I was haunted by the fear of being poor again, but also not enjoying success so much that I took my eye off the ball. Yes #BlackWomenDeserveRest but my attention to the business—as its visionary and leader—is critical to its success. I cannot be replaced by employees working on autopilot. What if when Teresa had called, I told her to give the customer what they wanted and went on about my business? What would have happened if I ignored that wriggling in my gut when I heard the strain in her voice? When would I have checked back in?

Would it have been too late? Where would that leave me? Babes was all I had.

Just reliving this makes my heart pound. According to the Bureau of Labor Statistics, 65 percent of businesses fail in their first ten years. Building longevity is especially important to those on the outside socioeconomically. When you come from nothing or have nothing, you have to build stability in the present while laying a foundation for the future. Part of me was annoyed by the weight that felt like it had resituated itself right on top of my shoulders. Hadn't I earned the right to coast for a while? Reaching the level of success that I'd attained had complicated the answer to that question *because* I came from nothing.

Over the years, I've found there are three common struggles that arise once someone has "arrived" on their success journey. How we respond to those obstacles will influence whether our success will last or phase out.

The first is *routine*. When Kim Kardashian started wearing my clothes, super pregnant with her first child, I could have amplified the moment on social media, pushed that dress to customers by highlighting it on my site, and left it at that. That dress in every color she wore sold out pretty much immediately. And it continued to sell out upon restocking. The nice thing about my design process at that time was that it didn't disrupt my routine. I had a flow of creating lines where I designed products, pulled fabrics, had samples made, then began marketing to build up to a big launch. I know so much about curvy women's bodies, I can size a woman by just looking at her. But when it came to putting my dresses on a pregnant woman, there were factors I didn't know how to grapple with. It required learning, altering my process, disrupting my routine a bit to get a good idea of how to properly size this outfit for maternity. I could choose to maintain my regular flow or branch out and do something different. Fortunately, I chose the latter and launched a maternity line. There was a learning curve, and I made some samples that had to be trashed, which cost me a bit of money. But the long-term benefit of understanding how to properly size a pregnant body was invaluable. And it allowed me to adapt to demand.

If you're stuck in a certain way of doing things, it can make you inflexible and resistant to adapting. Adapting is required when building success because the market, life, people, the world we live in are ever-evolving. The landscape of social selling is vastly different in 2024 than it was when I started in 2012. For starters, there's so much more competition. Adapting has enabled Babes to push through the noise and maintain its loyal customer base while keeping the brand invigorated with a splash of freshness. Sticking to the routine of adapting and evolving is good.

The second struggle is *growing unenthusiastic*. My first day back in the office full-time reminded me why I fell in love with fashion in the first place. I loved my job—being around the clothes was inspiring. But something had shifted in the last few years, little by little, and it was so subtle I'd missed it. And I realized it's what led to pants being sent out with slits not at all as I intended and customers feeling like I'd lost my ability to design. This was a problem that had been brewing for a long time. Somewhere between not designing vintage anymore and moving to production, I'd lost the thrill of putting together ideas and sketching fresh looks. Over the years, as Babes grew, my attention and focus moved to the business of running a business. I allocated less and less time, I realized, to the creative heart of my business. That heart was my fuel!

In those early years on Stacy's couch, a lot of my drive was the desperate desire to get out of poverty. But I can't ignore what brought me to LA in the first place: my love of fashion. Some of my fuel in those vintage thrifting years was putting surprising textures together, ripping apart fabrics and reworking them into something others couldn't imagine. Creating something different. Designing the vintage way was riskier. *Uncomfortable.* Moving to producing pieces was safer and a more efficient moneymaker. There is an inherent ease in the flow and process of doing one thing multiple times versus reinventing something new every time. I was still designing, scratching my creative itch as much as I could, but that whole process looked a bit different as a retailer. By this stage in my business, designing something wasn't a solitary process where I could be an ostrich and just stick my head in the sand and create whatever I wanted. As the brand grew, there were customer expectations to live up to, a brand identity to stick by, and a price point to consider. But those invigorating years of taking risks were where greatness appeared, playing around on the edge without worrying about the rest. I'm an outsider; the margins are where I'm invigorated and energized, and where I work my hardest and do my best! My heart wasn't in the core of my business as it once was and that was bleeding into my designs. Going back to vintage wasn't the answer. But I had to find my passion again.

When your passion for something you've had great success with dries up, you risk losing the hunger and drive that helped you get where you are in the first place. It's that passion that drives your creativity and work ethic. Keep it nourished!

—

The third struggle is *identity*. When I first started sharing clothes online, I posted them on my personal Instagram page. I didn't see the issue initially. My followers were interested in *me*, so I leveraged that interest into my clothes. Then my brand grew, my following increased, and posting pictures of myself wearing things—even random outfits I wasn't selling—was an implicit request for approval. I didn't see this at the time, but I later realized that when someone didn't like what I was wearing or commented negatively on a Babes product, they were effectively commenting on *me*— Ciera—because the lines between me as a person and the brand were so blurred. Those rejections felt crummy, like an attack on my personal sense of style, my talent, my vision. They would tempt me, at times, to question if I knew what I was doing at all, whether I'd lost my knack.

When your personal brand is your business, it's hard to be objective about how to improve if, as in my case, you see *yourself* every time you look at your business. If a particular project that you initially pioneered at work is now floundering, it can be difficult to evaluate that project impartially without reevaluating yourself. If you've built your personality and life around your job and then find yourself falling out of love with your career, what does that mean for your sense of self-worth and identity? If success for you is found in raising compassionate, well-adapted children to be meaningful contributors to society, then whenever you see the areas they still need to grow, it can be hard to not see those as a reflection of your own shortcomings.

Finding ways to improve the object of your success then becomes a gymnastics routine of evaluating *yourself.* It is dangerous to conflate yourself and your work. It is also insidious, often happening without you noticing. Starting Babes as my own personal brand wasn't wrong. In fact, many successful brands begin that way. But I needed to allow Babes to take on its own identity gradually. That project you spearheaded has taken its own wings as it's been molded and shaped by others along the way. Your children's pace of success, maturity, and growth is only within so much of your control. They are their own people! Take steps to consciously separate your self-perception from your work and where you put your focus so that you can objectively evaluate the next best step.

One way to do that is by resisting working all the time or pouring all of your identity into one thing like your job or parenting. If all you do is work or look after your children, you risk forgetting who you are outside of that. Keeping a sense of yourself outside all your other obligations—work, family, or friends—is key. If you're an entrepreneur like me, you need to find a strong work-life balance by rooting yourself firmly in who *you* are separate from your brand.

So what did I do?

With a heap of problems at my feet that first day back in the office, I knew quite immediately something had to change. And fast. That afternoon, I asked my team to stay late. As they gathered in the office, I could see the worry dug into lines on their faces. All they'd heard was "Ciera came in and flipped out." But I spent the bulk of our time together explaining that this was bigger than a few pants and unsatisfied customers. I took ownership over how I'd grown disengaged and how that was likely a long time coming, because my passion for the work I was doing was getting lost in the business of what I was doing. There were lots of nodding heads and darting eyes. It was important for me to let my team know how much I appreciated them sticking with the business, holding things together while I was out life-ing. And I made it clear I would be hands-on from then on.

It's a complex issue because I don't feel bad about living my life, getting absorbed in everyday things, and really inhaling financial *freedom* for the first time. But it was a wake-up call that I could not let the work-life pendulum swing too far in the other direction either. There had to be true balance. And the bottom line is my business does better when I'm passionate, hands-on, and engaged because it is that energy that built it in the first place. Babes thrives when I'm *not* comfortable.

That day in the warehouse, I went through and touched every single item of inventory I had. I spent that night combing through my sales, and I had my assistant pull a log of all my returns and sift through social media to find any displeased reviews. I wanted to keep track of just how far my being hands-off had shaped my business.

To my loyal customer who had essentially sparked my wake-up call, I sent a handwritten note of thanks for her loyalty. And various colors of a few of her favorite pieces. I also extended the invitation for her to sample my next design before it went to production. I told her she could try it on and give me her thoughts. It was important to me that she knew I heard her, I saw her, and I was reengaged. She'd helped save Babes, which I hadn't even realized needed saving.

With my customer and product issues taken care of, I turned to the bigger issue: me. I adjusted my processes. First, I amended my routine, starting my day with one nonnegotiable hour at the packing/inventory warehouse four times a week. I made a point to ensure I saw my employees and looked them in the face as often as possible. I also paid attention to items shipping out and items shipping back. Keeping a pulse on those things lets me know how my customers are feeling about pieces—which ones are working well, which ones may have some common issues. I do not ever assume "things are okay, so I can put my feet up." I make sure things are okay and *then* hop in the recliner.

To reinvigorate my passion, I harkened back to the early days of my business where I'd created vintage looks for curvy women that were unique and fresh. I was reinvigorated by the idea that I had been fixing a problem with my designs. So I brainstormed a big list of problems I wanted to address with future lines and the result was some of my bestselling lines to date. My no-back-gap jean was a favorite.

And to separate myself and my business, I made a point to continue living outside of work. I will not spend my entire day in the office anymore. I will make myself take a trip, go do things besides work, work, work. I love art. So I spend lots of time at galleries and shows, getting more and more in touch with who I am, separate from Babes. I also style myself like I used to, mixing and matching finds. I share these on my personal page, not my business page, to create some visual separation between the two. The styles I wear are very different from what Babes sells. And thankfully, little by little, it's getting easier to see where Babes ends and where I begin.

When you're carving out some new venture of success for yourself, you must give it your all. Once you've made a bit of progress, the desire to coast and just *be* comfortable can creep up on you and feel all too appealing. But your goals are rooted in big, important, generationally affecting things. You're revolutionizing your approach to self-care so that your children after you will engage in work in healthier ways by default. You're investing in land ownership so that you can build generational wealth. You're trying to build something that you and generations after you can stand on for a long time, which means the goal is not to become comfortable. Comfort can breed complacency. But outsiders are particularly skilled at embracing discomfort because being uncomfortable is a reality most of us must live with. We enter most spaces with the expectation of being uncomfortable. Before you're tempted to get grumpy about the fact that you can't get comfortable, don't miss the gem buried here. This means we are better equipped to perform, persist, and persevere *despite* discomfort.

This is a huge advantage. If you're trying to start a community garden in your neighborhood and that means speaking at community meetings, going door to door for support, and doing all kinds of extroverted things that make you want to break out in hives, this might feel uncomfortable, but that's fine. Perhaps you're trying to convince your boss that you're the best candidate for that lateral department transfer and you have to admit that you've been hunting for a different job *while* convincing them to recommend you. Sound comfortable? Probably not. But you got this. Being uncomfortable is growth.

Instead of placing the idea of comfort on a pedestal, make the goal finding balance between comfort and discomfort, recognizing that being somewhere on the pendulum is critical to success. You want to be on your toes the way you were in the beginning of your success journey, actively looking for ways to evolve as the landscape changes. Let's say you set a major health goal when you suddenly get a new job with unpredictable hours and lots of travel that could throw you off your plan to transform your health. Instead of giving up on these goals altogether, you need to find a new way to adapt your plan to the obstacles and changing conditions that arise. The pandemic was a great example of finding ways to adapt in an unexpected environment. We all learned to be flexible as we adjusted to a new reality, not seeing family, not leaving our homes, and working remotely. Be ready to pivot as problems crop up. You cannot adapt and evolve if you're riding the wave of comfort so hard that you aren't paying attention. You need to evolve and grow by embracing discomfort.

Comfort isn't the goal. A success that *lasts* is.

THE OUTSIDE SCOOP

I Memorialized the Successes I Had While Uncomfortable

I am constantly unimpressed with myself. This might seem odd considering the content of this book, but I promised you when we started this story that I would keep it completely honest. And the ugly truth is that when I look over all I've accomplished, my gut reaction is, "Meh, I did what I had to do." It took me years to really wrap my head around how to write this book because my brain wants me to think the stuff I've done is not a big deal. To combat this tendency, I began memorializing difficult moments where I was uncomfortable but found success and growth. I may make a detailed social post or pop a bottle of champagne to celebrate these moments. Sometimes I'll throw an entire party over something seemingly small that I overcame. These intentional celebrations cement the idea that being uncomfortable is where growth happens. It has remapped the way I think about being uncomfortable.

What discomfort are you running away from? Where are you hesitating in your journey toward success? How can you harness the feeling of being uncomfortable to your benefit?

14

Just Start Now

AFFIRMATION

*I will take at least one step
today to build the future
I envision for myself*

I once spoke to a woman who I was convinced would end up on some short list of brilliant, under-thirty millionaire entrepreneurs. Her name was Liselle. She was short and she didn't wear heels. *I* am short and I felt like I was towering over her. But she had a confidence to her energy that was magnetic. She hopped in line to talk with me after an event wrapped up. And when it was her turn, she shook my hand vigorously and introduced herself.

She then proceeded to detail an idea she had for revolutionizing how jewelry is marketed via direct sales. I reared back in my seat. I was accustomed to hearing others' entrepreneurial ideas. I get a dozen DMs a week from people—some friends, some strangers—who are bursting at the seams excited over their idea. Usually, they are curious if I have any advice. But Liselle's idea was so out of the box, I didn't know what to say at first. For the integrity and protection of her idea, I won't detail it here, because it isn't my concept to share. But trust me when I say Liselle was onto something *big*.

"When you get this off the ground," I said, "I will help you promote it. I have a whole network of resources I can share. This is brilliant."

Her tight lips pursed in a proud smile.

"Thank you, it's been a dream of mine for ten years."

"Where are you in the process?" I asked, leaning forward. *Did she need investors?*

"Oh, you mean have I started?"

I nodded and her bashful smile answered. She hadn't. I reiterated how impressed I was and gave her my contact info so she could keep in touch. I also got hers. Three months later, I still hadn't heard from Liselle, so I reached out to her. To my surprise, she responded quickly.

"Thanks for saying hi. But, no, I haven't been able to start yet. But I haven't forgotten what you said. I'm going to do it."

"You better!" was my reply.

She laughed and that's where the text chat ended.

I never heard from Liselle again.

I wish this experience with Liselle was uncommon, but I have met so many people over the years who are full of ideas. I can count on one hand how many of them ever put their idea into action.

Months later, I was at a bar waiting to meet friends, pondering this phenomenon further. Why weren't more brilliant ideas making it past the idea phase? I ordered a drink and eavesdropped on the conversation beside me. Two well-dressed men were celebrating one of them getting his father on board as an investor for some sort of real estate venture. Perhaps that was the problem for Liselle and so many others? Resources, be it time, money, or energy. But I told her I would share whatever resources I had. So it couldn't be that entirely. Liselle wasn't the only person I'd run into over the years who'd accepted my help to start something entrepreneurial but hadn't followed through. I'd spend hours on the phone with them, helping them troubleshoot their ideas. And then—nothing. They never did anything or followed up. And if I did, it was a dead end.

Resources may not be the reason you struggle to get started. It may be that you're hyperfocused on what could go wrong, so you are researching exhaustively. But are you doing that because it feels like an outcome you can control? There is something incredibly daunting about the unknown. It feels like a risk, a roll of the dice, and maybe you are averse to that. That could be your personality, or it could be situational for you as it was for me. I couldn't take many risks when I was on Stacy's couch. I just couldn't afford to expend resources and fail. But chasing dreams inherently involves risk. You can't ever control the outcome. But you can give yourself your best chance at success by putting into practice what we've outlined in this book. No amount of research is going to absolve you of risk. At some point, you have to just stop collecting information and get started.

Or perhaps you may be intimidated by the prospect of trying something and failing. It's as if, in your head, you've already accepted defeat. You can't know that you are going to fail any more than you can know you will succeed. If the fear of doing it wrong is stopping you, go back and reread chapter eleven. Failure is a part of success. You build *on* the foundation of failures to create something even more sturdy. Once you reframe failure as a part of creating success versus something to avoid at all costs, you'll begin to see pursuing your idea in a different light.

Or maybe you haven't started working toward the success you

dream of, be it a promotion at work or starting your own business, because you don't know where to start. Many are frozen with inaction because they don't know where to begin. I've felt it myself in writing this book. The idea of sharing my message and lessons was something I was so eager to do, and yet figuring out how to actually tell my story took years. I knew nothing about publishing or the craft of writing, and somehow, here we are. I heard a metaphor once that starting a big project feels like trying to figure out the best way to eat an elephant. If that's you, grab your knife and fork and cut it into smaller pieces. One step at a time. With each cut you will feel more capable. (Please don't go eat an elephant. This is a metaphor, people!) Before you know it, the next step feels doable.

I also have crossed paths with women who are comfortable in their routine and disrupting that to dive into a new endeavor isn't as desirable as it seems. To that person I say, girl, you have to want it badly and find it worth your time, or it isn't ever going to happen. Then there is the person with so many ideas they aren't sure which one to focus on. My friends and peers who fall in this category struggle with feeling like if they don't work on *all* their ideas, they'll lose them. That's not true! Make a portfolio of ideas in Google Docs or a journal with a new idea on each page. Choose *one*. Give that your focus for six months and see what happens.

The reasons people fail to put their ideas into action are endless, but you must realize that only *talking* about ideas is never going to bring them to fruition. The sure way to guarantee you will *not* be successful is to never try to be. You have to actually start. Some believe there are doers and talkers. I don't believe that, because the minute a talker puts the first step into action, their talking has turned them into a doer. Recognize if you are in this stalemate and take the first step to getting your success journey off the ground.

There is never going to be a perfect time when you're suddenly not busy or where you can focus completely on this new idea you have. If you wait for that moment, you will be waiting for a time that will never come. Time is also not guaranteed. You have today. Choose now.

All right, outsider, you've almost finished this book.

Sure, you could probably think of a bunch of reasons to not get started.

But you now *know* that you're uniquely equipped to build the success you crave.

And the time is now.

So, what are you going to do to get started?

THE OUTSIDE SCOOP

I Picked One Small, Noncommittal Step Forward

Commitment scares me. By now I'm sure you understand why. Deciding to take a step in the direction of some big lofty goal that I could fail at felt like a choke hold. Instead,

I decided to try one small thing without fully deciding if I'd take another step. Just to experience the trying. I wanted to see if the idea of becoming a fashion designer invigorated me like I thought it would. So before I designed anything, I created a dress by sketch and then perused some fabrics for it, imagining what it would look and feel like. I didn't cut anything. I didn't even buy anything. I just let myself wade in the idea and I knew right away that I wanted to take another step. Sometimes it's that easy to trick our brain to get out of our way.

ONE FINAL THING

By the time I was five years old, I'd been kidnapped by my father and stolen back by my mother. I'd lived with my younger sister on my mother's friend's mattress in a trailer. If you'd asked that Ciera who she would be when she grew up, she would have grinned at you and shrugged. If you asked her at fifteen years old, you'd probably get the same answer. I didn't know that I'd be a millionaire fashion designer living a dream in Los Angeles. But what I could tell you, even as a teenager, is that I was smart, ambitious, and tenacious. I could emphatically say that though I didn't know what my future would look like, I was certain that it wouldn't look like my past. I recognized that while my mother was doing the absolute best she could, I wanted more. And I knew, regardless of what it looked like on paper, I had what it took to be successful.

I would be successful even if I didn't know how.

Let's hang our hat here for a second. I want you to really breathe that in—it's okay to not know how. If you're on the first step of your success journey, commit to believing that you will be somewhere else at the end of this journey. That where you are right now is a stepping stone to where you will be. That whatever circumstances or experiences you had before this moment can be harnessed to build something you are proud of. Remember this moment right now, wherever you are reading or listening to this, as the moment that you committed to yourself. As the "before" moment when you decided to embark on your wild journey to success.

You have to start with knowing that you *can* succeed. After that comes the how.

Once you believe, take the first step by going through these chapters again, piece by piece, and giving yourself permission to sit with each one. Do not try to rush success. In book form, my success journey may seem like I was constantly moving and leveling up. But there were periods of nothing. Remember my strip club hustle? At one point, I was rigid with fear that that sort of hustling would be all I could accomplish. But it was only a season.

I've walked you through so many of my ups and downs to show you that life is a smattering of seasons. Seasons of growth, pruning, and yes, seasons of drought. You've had a sobering look at a few of mine. But despite the meandering, the waiting, the gaps of time where the word "success" felt like some dream I could never quite picture after I'd woken up, I was making my way, little by little, to a different reality. I was building success in layers, like the way you might build a sandcastle. First you have to gather the sand, then you form some of the larger structural pieces. And then you carefully and methodically build the bones of the castle. And finally, you work in the details.

As I mentioned when we ventured into this (awkwardly honest) exposé of my life, I told you this journey would not give you a road map to being rich. But there *is* a road map here. It's one that you have to draw in pencil with a big, fat eraser in hand. I want you to draw your own map, making sure to sketch the bumps in the road and the stretches of highway that seem to go in circles, and recognize that each and every one of those seeming delays is all part of your path to success.

My life was not a cakewalk. But it was filled with valuable lessons on resilience, optimism, and persistence. My path to creating the success in my life that I'd longed for wasn't paved with typical achievement milestones. There were no summers vacationing at a campsite, or winters skiing, or jet-setting across the pond to broaden my horizons of just how big this world is and experiencing all it has to offer. I didn't attend a private prep school or get a business degree from a top-ten-ranked university. I traipsed from one precarious situation to another on my mother's determination and love for her two daughters. And I made it work.

My success journey as an outsider didn't follow the prescribed path of those with stability and resources and connections. I meandered and backtracked. I made mistakes and failed a lot. But along the way, I took lessons with me about the person I was becoming *because* of those affective experiences. I dug into the mess of what I *did* have. I grabbed those memories you'd assume I'd want to forget, firmly with both hands, and used them to stitch a new reality from the thrifted fabrics of my life.

And it transformed a past that should have defeated me into a future that propelled me.

Now, it's your turn! I hope you're bursting at the seams with get-shit-done energy. Remember, there is power in being on the outside because

> you have untapped power,
>
> you have plenty to build from,
>
> you will be yourself,
>
> you are deserving of the very best in life,
>
> you are not alone,
>
> you will confidently and ethically tap into the wisdom and resources of the people you meet,
>
> you are successful if you are making progress toward your goals,
>
> you can learn to do anything,
>
> you will not feel guilty for leveling the playing field,
>
> you will use your past to build your future,
>
> you will survive your worst failures and be better because of them,
>
> you have a power that cannot be taken away,
>
> you didn't get this far by being comfortable and staying still, and
>
> you will take at least one step today to build the future you envision for yourself.

Now go step into the full power of your unique self and watch your life transform.

AFFIRMATIONS

1. I have untapped power

2. I have plenty to build from

3. I will be me

4. I am deserving of the very best in life

5. I am not alone

6. I will confidently and ethically tap into the wisdom and resources of the people I meet

7. If I am making progress toward my goals, I am successful

8. I can learn to do anything

9. I will not feel guilty for leveling the playing field

10. I will use my past to build my future

11. I will survive my worst failures and be better because of them

12. I have a power that cannot be taken away

13. I didn't get this far by being comfortable and staying still

14. I will take at least one step today to build the future I envision for myself

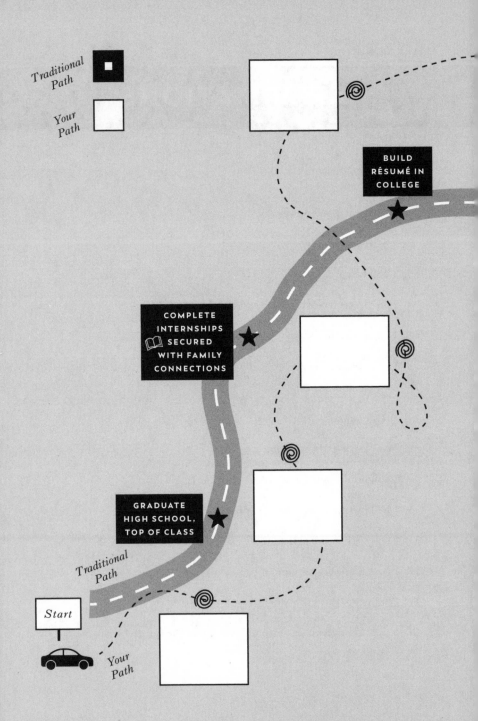

Traditional Path

Your Path

BUILD RÉSUMÉ IN COLLEGE

COMPLETE INTERNSHIPS SECURED WITH FAMILY CONNECTIONS

GRADUATE HIGH SCHOOL, TOP OF CLASS

Traditional Path

Start

Your Path

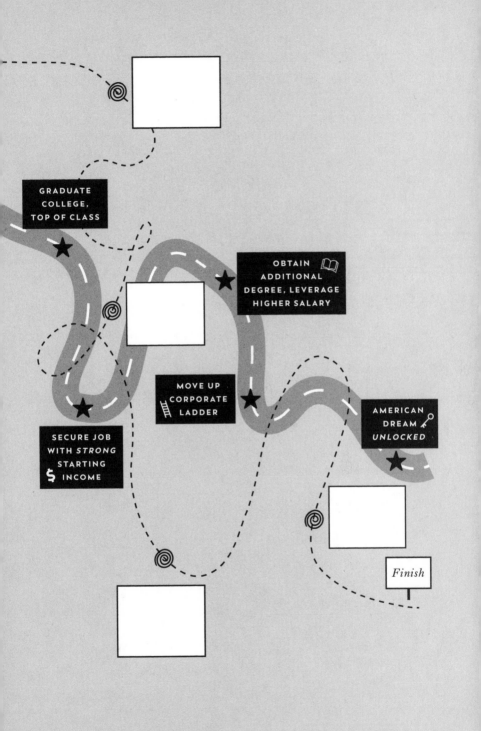

GRADUATE
COLLEGE,
TOP OF CLASS

OBTAIN
ADDITIONAL
DEGREE, LEVERAGE
HIGHER SALARY

MOVE UP
CORPORATE LADDER

AMERICAN
DREAM
UNLOCKED

SECURE JOB
WITH *STRONG*
STARTING
$ INCOME

Finish

ACKNOWLEDGMENTS

Thank you, Mom.

There aren't enough words or the right words to express all you mean to me. You made me what I am and who I am. Everything here, both the hard times and the good.

Christina if I could only spend the rest of my life with one person, I would choose you every time. You inspire me every single day. Love you, sis. To Donte, you've been my support system and ultimate teammate. Jessica, thanks for convincing me to pursue a book deal and cowriting this book with me. I've admired you since that first day I saw you walking in that LECJ hallway. Thank you to my BABES, my customers who have supported me throughout the years. I am so grateful! To Teresa, thank you for running Babes like it's yours, helping me with Mom like she's your own, and treating me like family. We are in this together, always.

Uncle Paulfry, you are the best and I am so grateful for you. You've shown me what a father is supposed to look like. I love you! Thank you, Rick Lowe, for changing our lives with the free house. You are forever family. Thank you, Adrian, Lydia, Leah T., Nina, Niki, and the entire Portfolio team for seeing what this book could be and sticking with us to get it done. A special shout-out to

Lydia for supporting me while I spiraled on several occasions. I know editors don't usually text their authors as much as you did. I appreciate you! Thank you to my agent, Natalie, who believed in this from the very beginning. Jeannine, thank you for the long chats and the astute notes. I learned so much with your help. Sending you and your daughter so much love.

And a very special thanks to *all* the people over the years who refused to give me a job. You forced me to realize what I could do on my own.

Finally, thank you to readers, who took the time to read this deeply personal, occasionally awkward (for me) life story. I hope the person you see in the mirror looks a bit different now. Because you finally see all that's there. ♥

Now go smash the patriarchy and do epic shit.

INDEX